ALSO BY ROBERT KAGAN

*Dangerous Nation: America's Place in the World from Its
Earliest Days to the Dawn of the Twentieth Century*

*Of Paradise and Power: America and Europe
in the New World Order*

*A Twilight Struggle:
American Power and Nicaragua, 1977-1990*

*Present Dangers: Crisis and Opportunity in
American Foreign and Defense Policy*
(edited with William Kristol)

THE RETURN
OF HISTORY
AND THE END
OF DREAMS

THE RETURN OF HISTORY AND THE END OF DREAMS

ROBERT KAGAN

Alfred A. Knopf

NEW YORK   2008

THIS IS A BORZOI BOOK
PUBLISHED BY ALFRED A. KNOPF

Copyright © 2008 by Robert Kagan

All rights reserved. Published in the United States by
Alfred A. Knopf, a division of Random House, Inc.,
New York, and in Canada by Random House of
Canada Limited, Toronto.

www.aaknopf.com

Knopf, Borzoi Books, and the colophon are registered
trademarks of Random House, Inc.

Material in this work is taken from and based upon the article
"End of Dreams, Return of History" by Robert Kagan, which
originally appeared in *Policy Review.*

Library of Congress Control Number: 2008922338

Manufactured in the United States of America

First Edition

For Dad

THE RETURN
OF HISTORY
AND THE END
OF DREAMS

THE WORLD HAS BECOME normal again. The years immediately following the end of the Cold War offered a tantalizing glimpse of a new kind of international order, with nation-states growing together or disappearing, ideological conflicts melting away, cultures intermingling, and increasingly free commerce and communications. The modern democratic world wanted to believe that the end of the Cold War did not just end one strategic and ideological conflict but all strategic and ideological conflict. People and their leaders longed for "a world transformed."[1]

But that was a mirage. The world has not been transformed. In most places, the nation-state remains as strong as ever, and so, too, the nationalist ambitions, the passions, and the competition among nations that have shaped history. The United States remains the sole superpower. But international competition among great powers has returned, with Russia, China, Europe, Japan, India, Iran, the United States, and others vying for regional predominance. Struggles for status and influence in the world have returned as central features of the international scene. The old competition between liberalism and autocracy has also reemerged, with the world's great powers increasingly lining up according to the nature of their regimes. And an even older struggle has erupted between radical Islamists and the modern secular cultures and powers that they believe have dominated, penetrated, and polluted their Islamic world. As these three struggles combine and collide, the promise of a new era of international convergence fades. We have entered an age of divergence.

With the dreams of the post–Cold War era dissolving, the democratic world will have to decide how to respond. In recent years, as the autocracies of Russia and China have risen and the radical Islamists have waged their struggle, the democracies have been divided and distracted by issues both profound and petty. They have questioned their purpose and their morality, argued over power and ethics, and pointed to one another's failings. Disunity has weakened and demoralized the democracies at a moment when they can least afford it. History has returned, and the democracies must come together to shape it, or others will shape it for them.

HOPES AND DREAMS

IN THE EARLY 1990S, the optimism was understandable and almost universal. The collapse of the communist empire and the apparent embrace of democracy by Russia seemed to augur a new era of global convergence. The great adversaries of the Cold War suddenly shared many common goals, including a desire for economic and political integration. Even after the political crackdown that began in Tiananmen Square in 1989 and disturbing signs of instability in Russia after 1993, most Americans and Europeans believed China and Russia were on a path toward liberalism. Boris Yeltsin's Russia seemed committed to the liberal model of political economy and closer integration with the West. The Chinese government's commitment to economic opening, it was hoped, would inevitably produce a political opening, whether Chinese leaders wanted it or not.

Such determinism was characteristic of post–Cold War thinking. In a globalized economy, most believed, nations had no choice but to liberalize, first economically, then politically, if they wanted to compete and survive. As national economies approached a certain level of per capita income, growing middle classes would demand legal and political power, which rulers would have to grant if they wanted their nations to prosper. Since democratic capitalism was the most successful model for developing societies, all societies would eventually choose that path. In the battle of ideas, liberalism had triumphed. As Francis Fukuyama famously put it, "At the end of history, there are no serious ideological competitors left to liberal democracy."[2]

The economic and ideological determinism of the early post–Cold War years produced two broad assumptions that shaped both policies and expectations. One was an abiding belief in the inevitability of human progress, the belief that history moves in only one direction— a faith born in the Enlightenment, dashed by the brutality of the twentieth century, but given new life by the fall of communism. The other was a prescription for patience and restraint. Rather than confront and challenge autocracies, it was better to enmesh them in the global economy, support the rule of law and the creation of stronger state institutions, and let the ineluctable forces of human progress work their magic.

With the world converging around the shared principles of Enlightenment liberalism, the great task of the post–Cold War era was to build a more perfect international system of laws and institutions, fulfilling the prophecies of Enlightenment thought stretching back to the seventeenth and eighteenth centuries. A world of liberal governments would be a world without war, just as Kant had imagined. The free flow of both goods and ideas in the new globalized era would be an antidote to human conflict. As Montesquieu had argued, "The natural effect of commerce is to lead toward peace."[3] This old Enlightenment dream seemed suddenly possible because, along with the apparent triumph of international liberalism, the geopolitical and strategic interests of the world's great powers also seemed to converge. In 1991, President George H. W. Bush spoke of a "new world order" in which "the nations of the world, East and West, North and South, can prosper and live in harmony," where "the rule of law supplants the rule of the jungle," where nations "recognize the shared responsibility for freedom and justice." It was "a world quite different from the one we've known."[4]

The world looked different primarily because the Soviet Union was different. No one would have suggested that history had ended if the communist Soviet Union had not so suddenly and dramatically died and been transformed after 1989. The transformation of Soviet and then Russian foreign policy was remarkable. The "peaceful influence of liberal ideas" completely reoriented Russian perspectives on the world—or so it seemed.[5] Even in the last years of the Cold War, advocates of "new thinking" in Moscow called for convergence and the breakdown of barriers between East and West, a common embrace, as Mikhail Gorbachev put it, of "universal values." Then, in the early Yeltsin years, under foreign minister Andrei Kozyrev, Russia appeared committed to entering postmodern Europe. Moscow no longer defined its interests in terms of territory and traditional spheres of interest but rather in terms of economic integration and political development. It renounced regional hegemony, withdrew troops from neighboring states, slashed defense budgets, sought alliance with the European powers and the United States, and in general shaped its foreign policies on the premise that its interests were the same as those of the West. Russia's "wish was simply to belong."[6]

The democratization of Russia, beginning even in the Gorbachev years, had led the country's leaders to redefine and recalculate Russia's national interests. Moscow could give up imperial control in Eastern Europe, could give up its role as a superpower, not because the strategic situation had changed—if anything, the United States was more menacing in 1985 than it had been in 1975—but because the regime in Moscow had changed. A democratizing Russia did not fear the United States or the enlargement of its alliance of democracies.[7]

If Russia could abandon traditional great power politics, so could the rest of the world. "The age of geopolitics has given way to an age of what might be called geo-economics," Martin Walker wrote in 1996. "The new virility symbols are exports and productivity and growth rates and the great international encounters are the trade pacts of the economic superpowers."[8] Competition among nations might continue, but it would be peaceful commercial competition. Nations that traded with one another would be less likely to fight one another. Increasingly commercial societies would be more liberal both at home and abroad. Their citizens would seek prosperity and comfort and abandon the atavistic passions, the struggles for honor and glory, and the tribal hatreds that had produced conflict throughout history.

The ancient Greeks believed that embedded in human nature was something called *thumos,* a spiritedness and ferocity in defense of clan, tribe, city, or state. In the Enlightenment view, however, commerce would tame and perhaps even eliminate *thumos* in people and in nations. "Where there is commerce," Montesquieu wrote, "there are soft manners and morals."[9] Human nature could be improved, with the right international structures, the right politics, and the right economic systems. Liberal democracy did not merely constrain natural human instincts for aggression and violence; Fukuyama argued it "fundamentally transformed the instincts themselves."[10]

The clash of traditional national interests was a thing of the past, therefore. The European Union, the political scientist Michael Mandelbaum speculated, was but "a foretaste of the way the world of the twenty-first century [would] be organized."[11] The liberal internationalist scholar G. John Ikenberry described a post–Cold War world in which "democracy and markets flourished around the world, globalization was enshrined as a progressive historical force, and ideology, nationalism and war were at a low ebb." It was the triumph of "the liberal vision of international order."[12]

For Americans, the fall of the Soviet Union seemed a heaven-sent chance to fulfill a long-held dream of global leadership—a leadership welcomed and even embraced by the world. Americans had always considered themselves the world's most important nation and its destined leader. "The cause of America is the cause of all mankind," Benjamin Franklin said at the time of the Revolution. The United States was the "locomotive at the head of mankind," Dean Acheson said at the dawn of the Cold War, with the rest of the world merely "the caboose." After the Cold War it was still "the indispensable nation," indispensable because it alone had the power and the understanding necessary to help bring the international community together in common cause.[13] In the new world order, as Deputy Secretary of State Strobe Talbott put it, the United States would define "its strength—indeed, its very greatness—not in terms of its ability to achieve or maintain dominance over others, but in terms of its ability to work *with* others in the interests of the international community as a whole."[14]

While Americans saw their self-image reaffirmed by the new world order, Europeans believed that the new international order would be modeled after the European Union. As scholar-diplomat Robert Cooper put it, Europe was leading the world into a postmodern age, in which traditional national interests and power politics would give way to international law, supranational institutions, and pooled sovereignty. The cultural, ethnic, and nationalist divisions that had plagued mankind, and Europe, would be dissolved by shared values and shared economic interests. The EU, like the United States, was expansive, but in a postmodern way. Cooper envisioned the enlarging union as a kind of voluntary empire. Past empires had imposed their laws and systems of government. But in the post–Cold War era, "no one is imposing anything." Nations were eager to join the EU's "cooperative empire ... dedicated to liberty and democracy." A "voluntary movement of self-imposition [was] taking place."[15]

Even as these hopeful expectations arose, however, there were clouds on the horizon, signs of global divergence, stubborn traditions of culture, civilization, religion, and nationalism that resisted or cut against the common embrace of democratic liberalism and market capitalism. The core assumptions of the post–Cold War years collapsed almost as soon as they were formulated.

THE RETURN OF
GREAT POWER NATIONALISM

THE HOPES FOR A NEW ERA in human history rested on a unique set of international circumstances: the temporary absence of traditional great power competition. For centuries, the struggle among great powers for influence, wealth, security, status, and honor had been the main source of conflict and war. For more than four decades during the Cold War, the jostling had been limited to the two superpowers; their rigid bipolar order suppressed the normal tendency of other great powers to emerge. When the Soviet Union collapsed in 1991, suddenly only the United States remained. Russia was weak, its morale low, its domestic politics in turmoil, its economy in receivership, its military power in sharp decline. China, after the events at Tiananmen Square, was isolated, nervous, and introspective, its economic future uncertain, and its military unprepared for modern high-tech warfare. Japan, the rising economic superpower of the 1980s, had suffered a calamitous stock market crash in 1990 and was entering a decade of economic contraction. India had not yet begun its own economic revolution. And Europe, that premier arena of great power competition, was rejecting power politics and perfecting its postmodern institutions.

Geopolitical realists like Henry Kissinger warned at the time that this set of circumstances could not last, that international competition was embedded in human nature and would return. And although predictions of an imminent global multipolarity—with the United States, China, Russia, Japan, and India all roughly equal in power—proved mistaken, the realists had a clearer understanding of the unchanging nature of human beings. The world was witnessing not a transformation but merely a pause in the endless competition of nations and peoples.

Over the course of the 1990s, that competition re-emerged as, one by one, rising powers entered or reentered the field. First China, then India, set off on unprecedented bursts of economic growth, accompanied by incremental but substantial increases in military capacity, both conventional and nuclear. By the beginning of the twenty-first century, Japan had begun a slow economic recovery and was moving toward a more active international role both diplomatically and militarily. Then came Russia, rebounding from economic calamity to steady growth built on export of its huge reserves of oil and natural gas.

Today, a new configuration of power is reshaping the international order. It is a world of "one superpower, many great powers," as the Chinese strategists put it.[16] Nationalism and the nation itself, far from being weakened by globalization, have now returned with a vengeance. Ethnic nationalisms continue to bubble up in the Balkans and in the former republics of the Soviet Union. But more significant is the return of great power nationalism. Instead of a new world order, the clashing interests and ambitions of the great powers are again producing the alliances and counteralliances, and the elaborate dances and shifting partnerships, that a nineteenth-century diplomat would recognize instantly. They are also producing geopolitical fault lines where the ambitions of great powers overlap and conflict and where the seismic events of the future are most likely to erupt.

THE RISE OF RUSSIA

ONE OF THESE FAULT LINES runs along the western and southwestern frontiers of Russia. In Georgia, Ukraine, and Moldova, in the Baltic states of Estonia, Latvia, and Lithuania, in Poland, Hungary, and the Czech Republic, in the Caucasus and Central Asia, and even in the Balkans, a contest for influence is under way between a resurgent Russia on one side, and the European Union and the United States on the other. Instead of an anticipated zone of peace, western Eurasia has once again become a zone of competition.

If Russia was where history most dramatically ended two decades ago, today it is where history has most dramatically returned. Russia's turn toward liberalism at home stalled and then reversed, and so has its foreign policy. The centralization of power in the hands of Vladimir Putin has been accompanied by a turn away from the integrationist foreign policy championed by Yeltsin and Kozyrev. Great power nationalism has returned to Russia, and with it traditional great power calculations and ambitions.

Contrary to the dismissive views of many in the West, Russia is a great power, and it takes pride in being a force to be reckoned with on the world stage. It is not a superpower, and may never again be one. But in terms of what the Chinese call "comprehensive national power"—its combined economic, military, and diplomatic strengths— Russia ranks among the strongest powers in the world today. Its economy, after shrinking throughout most of the 1990s, has been growing by 7 percent annually since 2003 and seems likely to continue growing in the years to come. Between 1998 and 2006, the overall size of the Russian economy increased by more than 50 percent, real income per capita grew by 65 percent, and poverty rates were cut in half.

Much of this growth has been due to record high

prices for oil and gas, which Russia possesses in abundance. Russia holds the greatest reserves of mineral resources of any country in the world, including the largest reserves of petroleum and nearly half of the world's potential coal reserves. As a result, Russia enjoys a sizable trade and current-accounts surplus, has paid off almost all its foreign debt, and holds the world's third-largest hard currency reserves.[17]

It is not just that Russia is wealthier. It has something that other nations need—and need desperately. Europe now depends more on Russia for its supply of energy than on the Middle East. In theory, of course, Russia depends on the European market as much as the European market depends on Russia. But in practice Russians believe they are in the driver's seat, and Europeans seem to agree. Russian businesses, in close cooperation with the central government in Moscow, are buying up strategic assets across Europe, especially in the energy sectors, thereby gaining political and economic influence and tightening Russian control over European energy supply and distribution.[18] European governments fear that Moscow can manipulate the flow of energy supplies, and Russian leaders know this gives them the means to compel European acquiescence to Russian behavior that Europeans would not have tolerated in the past, when Russia was weak. Russia can now play European nations off against one another, dividing and thus blunting an EU that is less coherent and powerful than its proponents would like, even on economic and trade matters. As the EU commissioner for trade, Peter Mandelson, has complained, "No other country reveals our differences as does Russia."[19]

Russia is not only an economic power. Although it possesses a fraction of America's military capabilities, its oil and gas wealth has allowed Moscow to increase defense spending by more than 20 percent annually over the past three years. Today it spends more than every country in the world except for the United States and China. Much of this has gone to modernizing its nuclear arsenal, which remains formidable by any standard—Russia still possesses 16,000 nuclear warheads. But Russia also has an active-duty force of more than a million soldiers; is developing new jet fighters, new submarines, and new aircraft carriers; and has resumed long-range strategic bomber flights for the first time since the end of the Cold War. Russian military power, moreover, is an integral part of its foreign policy. In addition to fighting a war in Chechnya, it maintains troops in Georgia and Moldova and has suspended its participation in the Treaty on Conventional Armed Forces in Europe (CFE), which had restricted its troop deployments. It has also been the leading supplier of advanced weaponry to China and has thus made itself a factor in the strategic equation of East Asia.

Power is the ability to get others to do what you want and prevent them from doing what you don't want. With its natural resources, its disposable wealth, its veto at the United Nations Security Council, and its influence across Eurasia, Russia has made itself a player on every international issue, from the strategic architecture of Europe to the oil politics of Central Asia to the nuclear proliferation policies of Iran and North Korea.

This new sense of power today fuels Russian nationalism. It also stirs up deep resentments and feelings of humiliation. Russians today no longer regard Moscow's accommodating policies in the 1990s as acts of enlightened statesmanship. The acceptance of NATO enlargement; the withdrawal of troops from former Soviet republics; the ceding of independence to Ukraine, Georgia, and the Baltic states; the acceptance of a growing American and European influence in Central Europe, the Caucasus, and Central Asia—today Russians consider the post–Cold War settlement as nothing more than a surrender imposed by the United States and Europe at a time of Russian weakness.

Some Russian observers point to the enlargement of NATO and the war over Kosovo as the great catalysts for Russian revanchism.[20] But Russian resentments and sense of humiliation run deeper than this. When Putin called the collapse of the Soviet Union "the greatest geopolitical catastrophe of the century," he shocked the liberal West but struck a chord with Russians. It is not that they yearn for a return to Soviet communism— though there has been a remarkable resurrection of even Joseph Stalin's reputation.[21] Rather, they yearn for the days when Russia was respected by others and capable of influencing the world and safeguarding the nation's interests. The mood of recrimination in Russia today is reminiscent of Germany after World War I, when Germans complained about the "shameful Versailles diktat" imposed on a prostrate Germany by the victorious powers, and about the corrupt politicians who stabbed the nation in the back.

Today Russia's leaders seek to reclaim much of the global power and influence they lost at the end of the Cold

War. Their grand ambition is to undo the post–Cold War settlement and to reestablish Russia as a dominant power in Eurasia, to make it one of the two or three great powers of the world.

This is not quite what the western democracies hoped for or expected in the 1990s. They believed they were being more than generous when they offered to welcome Russia into the European home and into their international political and economic institutions after the Cold War. The billions of dollars in foreign assistance the West provided to Russia in the 1990s were a far cry from the huge sums the victorious powers tried to extract from Germany after 1918.

Russia's increasingly nationalist leadership, however, is no longer content to be invited into the western club on the same terms as any other nation. As Dmitri Trenin puts it, Russia would be willing to join the West only "if it was given something like co-chairmanship of the Western club" and could take its "rightful place in the world alongside the United States and China."[22] Russian leaders today yearn not for integration in the West but for a return to a special Russian greatness.

Lord Palmerston once observed that nations have no permanent friends, only permanent interests. But a nation's perceptions of its interests are not fixed. They change as perceptions of power change. With new power come new ambitions, or the return of old ones, and this is true not just of Russia but of all nations. International relations theorists talk about "status quo" powers, but nations are never entirely satisfied. When one horizon has been crossed, a new horizon always beckons. What was once unimaginable becomes imaginable, and then desirable. Desire becomes ambition, and ambition becomes interest. More powerful nations are not necessarily more contented nations. They may actually be less contented.

Russia's ambitions in recent years have grown outward in concentric circles. In the late 1990s and in the first years of the new century, Prime Minister and then President Putin was preoccupied with reestablishing the coherence and stability of the Russian Federation, including in the once defiant republic of Chechnya. As he has gradually succeeded in crushing the rebellion in Chechnya, he has directed Russian energies outward to the "near abroad" and Eastern Europe in an effort to reassert Russian influence in these traditional spheres of interest.

This requires reversing the pro-western trends of the past decades. In 2003 and 2004, when pro-western governments replaced pro-Russian governments in Ukraine and Georgia, thanks in part to significant financial and diplomatic support from the European Union and the United States, the strategic ramifications for Russia were clear and troubling. The leaders of Ukraine sought greater independence from Moscow, as well as membership in the European Union. The president of Georgia soon sought to join NATO. Even tiny Moldova took a more pro-western course. Together with the Baltic states of Lithuania, Estonia, and Latvia, these former Soviet republics now formed a belt of independent and potentially pro-western states up and down the length of Russia's western border. What the West called the "color revolutions" (the "orange revolution" in Ukraine, the "rose revolution" in Georgia, the "tulip revolution" in Kyrgyzstan) made Russians anxious about their declining influence in the "near abroad."[23]

Russia once tolerated these developments, perhaps because it had no choice. But today things are different. Having failed to prevent the incorporation of the Baltic states into NATO and the EU, Moscow is bent on preventing Georgia and Ukraine from joining or even being invited to join. Having lost its former Warsaw Pact allies to the American-led alliance, Russian leaders now want to carve out a special zone of security within NATO, with a lesser status for countries along its strategic flanks. That is the primary motive behind Russia's opposition to American missile defense programs in Poland and the Czech Republic. It is not only that Russians fear the proposed sites may someday threaten their nuclear strike capacity: Putin has suggested placing the sites in Italy, Turkey, or France instead. He wants to turn Poland and other eastern members of NATO into a strategic neutral zone.

What Russia wants today is what great powers have always wanted: to maintain predominant influence in the regions that matter to them, and to exclude the influence of other great powers. Were Russia to succeed in establishing this regional dominance, like other great powers its ambitions would expand. When the United States made itself the dominant power in the Western Hemisphere at the end of the nineteenth century, it did not rest content but looked to new horizons in East Asia and the Pacific. Russia's self-image today is that of a world power, with global interests and global reach.

Russia and the EU are neighbors geographically. But geopolitically they live in different centuries. A twenty-first-century EU, with its noble ambition to transcend power politics and lead the world into a new international order based on laws and institutions, now confronts a Russia that is very much a traditional, nineteenth-century power practicing the old power politics. Both are shaped by their histories. The postmodern, "post-national" spirit of the European Union was Europe's response to the horrific conflicts of the twentieth century, when nationalism and power politics twice destroyed the continent. Russian foreign policy attitudes have been shaped by the perceived failure of "post-national politics" after the collapse of the Soviet Union. Europe's nightmares are the 1930s; Russia's nightmares are the 1990s. Europe sees the answer to its problems in transcending the nation-state and power. For Russians, the solution is in restoring them.[24]

So what happens when a twenty-first-century entity like the EU faces the challenge of a traditional power like Russia? The answer will play itself out in coming years, but the contours of the conflict are already emerging—in diplomatic standoffs over Kosovo, Ukraine, Georgia, and Estonia; in conflicts over gas and oil pipelines; in nasty diplomatic exchanges between Russia and Great Britain; and in a return of Russian military exercises of a kind not seen since the Cold War.

Europeans are apprehensive and have reason to be. The nations of the European Union placed a mammoth bet in the 1990s. They bet on the new world order, on the primacy of geo-economics over geopolitics, in which a huge and productive European economy would compete as an equal with the United States and China. They transferred much of their economic and political sovereignty to strengthen EU institutions in Brussels. They cut back on their defense budgets and slowed the modernization of their militaries, calculating that soft power was in and hard power was out. They believed Europe would be a model for the world, and in a world modeled after the European Union, Europe would be strong.

For a while, this seemed a good bet. The European Union exerted a powerful magnetic force, especially on the states around it. It was a continent-sized island of relative stability in a global ocean of turmoil. With Russia prostrate, the attraction of Europe, along with the promise of the American security guarantee, pulled just about every nation to the east into the western orbit. Former Warsaw Pact nations, led by Poland, Hungary, and the Czech Republic, entered the EU, along with the Baltic states. The gravitational pull of Europe shaped politics in Ukraine and Georgia, as well as in Turkey. The appeal of Europe's liberal "voluntary empire" seemed without limit.

In recent years, however, the expansion of the voluntary empire has slowed. The enlargement of the EU to twenty-seven members has given the original EU members indigestion, and the looming prospect of taking in Turkey, with its 80 million Muslims, is more than many Europeans can stand. But the halt in EU enlargement is not only about fear of Turks and the "Polish plumber." When the EU brought in the former Warsaw Pact states and the Baltics, it acquired not only new eastern countries but also a new eastern problem. Or rather, it was the old eastern problem, the age-old contest between Russia and its near neighbors. When the EU ingested Poland, it also ingested Poland's enmity and suspicion of Russia (and of Germany). When it took in the Baltics, it took in their fear of Russia, as well as the large minority Russian populations within their borders.

These problems seemed manageable so long as Russia was moving along its postmodern, integrationist path, or at least so long as it was weak, poor, and absorbed by internal difficulties. But with Russia back on its feet and seeking to restore its great power status, including predominance in its traditional spheres of influence, Europe finds itself in a most unexpected and unwanted position of geopolitical competition. This great twenty-first-century entity has, through enlargement, embroiled itself in a very nineteenth-century confrontation.

Europe may be ill-equipped to respond to a problem that it never anticipated having to face. Its postmodern tools of foreign policy were not designed to address more traditional geopolitical challenges. The foreign policy of enlargement has stalled, and perhaps stalled permanently, partly because of Russia. Many western Europeans already regret having brought the eastern European countries into the Union and are unlikely to seek even more confrontations with Russia by admitting such states as Georgia and Ukraine.

Europe is neither institutionally nor temperamentally prepared to play the kind of geopolitical games in Russia's near-abroad that Russia is willing to play. Against Europe's powerful attractive force, Russia has responded using old-fashioned forms of power to punish or unseat pro-western leaders. It has imposed a total embargo on trade with Georgia. It has episodically denied oil supplies to Lithuania, Latvia, and Belarus; cut off gas supplies to Ukraine and Moldova; and punished Estonia with a suspension of rail traffic and a cyber attack on its government's computer system in a dispute over a Soviet war memorial. French president Nicolas Sarkozy bluntly observed that "Russia is imposing its return on the world scene by playing its assets, notably oil and gas, with a certain brutality."[25] These are foreign policy tools that the EU probably could not use, even if some of its members wanted to.[26]

Nor will the EU match Russia's use of military tools. Moscow supports separatist movements in Georgia and keeps its own armed forces on Georgian territory and in Moldova. It threatens to withdraw entirely from the CFE Treaty, negotiated back in the 1990s, so that it will be freer to deploy forces wherever necessary up and down its western flank. Even the Finnish defense minister worries that "military force" has once again become a "key element" in how Russia "conducts its international relations."[27] Europeans increasingly take a dim view of the great power on their eastern borders and of the weapons it deploys to pursue its interests.[28] But would Europe bring a knife to a knife fight?

It is not hard to imagine the tremors along the Euro-Russian fault line erupting into confrontation. A crisis over Ukraine, which wants to join NATO, could provoke Russian belligerence. Conflict between the Georgian government and separatist forces in Abkhazia and South

Ossetia supported by Russia could spark a military conflict between Tbilisi and Moscow. What would Europe
and the United States do if Russia played hardball in either
Ukraine or Georgia? They might well do nothing. Postmodern Europe can scarcely bring itself to contem-
plate a return of conflict involving a great power and will
go to great lengths to avoid it. Nor is the United States
eager to take on Russia when it is so absorbed in the
Middle East. Nevertheless, a Russian confrontation with
Ukraine or Georgia would usher in a brand-new world—
or rather a very old world. As one Swedish analyst has
noted, "We're in a new era of geopolitics. You can't pretend
otherwise."[29]

How contrary to the perceptions and expectations of
the post–Cold War era. In the 1990s, the democracies
expected that a wealthier Russia would be a more liberal
Russia, at home and abroad. But historically the spread of
commerce and the acquisition of wealth by nations has
not necessarily produced greater global harmony. Often it
has only spurred greater global competition. The hope at
the end of the Cold War was that nations would pursue
economic integration as an alternative to geopolitical
competition, that they would seek the soft power of commercial engagement and economic growth as an alternative to the hard power of military strength or geopolitical
confrontation. But nations do not need to choose. There is
another paradigm—call it "rich nation, strong army," the
slogan of rising Meiji Japan at the end of the nineteenth
century—in which nations seek economic integration
and adaptation of western institutions not in order to give

up the geopolitical struggle but as a way of waging it more successfully.

THE RISE OF CHINA

THE CHINESE HAVE THEIR OWN PHRASE for this: "prosperous country and a strong army."[30] Sixty years ago, China was on its back, torn by domestic conflict, invaded, occupied, vulnerable, poor, isolated. Today, it is a rising geopolitical and economic giant, secure within its borders. Its economy is racing to become the largest in the world. Its military power is steadily growing. Its political influence is expanding apace with its economic and military power. Perhaps no nation has ever moved further faster from weakness to strength.

Power changes people, and it changes nations. It changes their perceptions of themselves, of their interests, of their proper standing in the world, of how they expect to be treated by others. That is why the rise of great powers throughout history has so often produced tensions in the international system, and even great wars. The ancient Egyptians, Persians, and Greeks; the Romans, Franks, Ottomans, and Venetians; the French, Spanish, British, Russians, Germans, Americans, and Japanese—all struggled and fought with varying degrees of success to open space for themselves in the world as befit their growing economic and military power, and to shape the world in accord with their perceived interests and their beliefs.

In the age of optimism that followed the Cold War,

the hope was that China would take a different course. Because mankind had entered a new era of globalization and interdependence, because the old geopolitics and its power competitions had given way to the new geo-economics with its imperative of cooperation, many expected that a nation like China could rise without violently challenging the international order. Instead of "zero-sum," China's relations with the world would be "win-win."

This is certainly how the Chinese wanted to be perceived. As the Chinese scholar and Communist Party theorist Zheng Bijian put it a few years ago, China would "not follow the path of Germany leading up to World War I or those of Germany and Japan leading up to World War II," or of "the great powers vying for global domination during the Cold War." It would "transcend the traditional ways for great powers to emerge" and "strive for peace, development, and cooperation with all countries of the world."[31]

The democracies sought to manage China's rise by engaging it economically and diplomatically, entwining it in a thick web of commercial ties, and welcoming its involvement in international trade and political regimes, all in an effort to facilitate its transcendence of traditional power politics and steer it into a safe, twenty-first-century postmodern existence.

In some respects, the strategy has been successful. China's increasing involvement in and dependence on the global economy has indeed made it a more "responsible stakeholder" in the international economic system and a fairly cautious player, so far, on the international scene.

The Chinese have developed an interest in the well-being of the global economy, and particularly of the American economy, on which China relies for its life's blood.

But it is not so easy to escape history, and in other important ways China has behaved like rising powers before it.

China's booming economy has not only involved China in the world. It has given the Chinese people and their leaders a new confidence, a new pride, and a not unreasonable feeling that the future belongs to them. Their newfound economic prowess has revived old feelings of what Americans would call manifest destiny, a deeply rooted belief that China has been before and will be again a central force in the world. For more than a millennium China was the dominant power in Asia, the only advanced civilization in a world of barbarians, the center of its own universe, both spiritually and geopolitically the Middle Kingdom. In the early nineteenth century, the Chinese found themselves prostrate, "thrown out to the margins" of a suddenly Eurocentric world.[32] The "century of humiliation" that ensued was so shameful because China's fall came from such a glorious height.

Today the Chinese believe that their nation's ancient centrality, appropriately adjusted for the times and circumstances, can, should, and will be restored.[33] They increasingly look back to imperial days for guidance about the future.[34] Chinese thinkers and policymakers foresee a dawning era of renewed Chinese dominance in East Asia. Some see the world divided into two geopolitical spheres: a Euro-Atlantic sphere dominated by the United States and an Asian sphere dominated by China. Others see the world divided into three monetary zones: the dollar, the euro, and the Chinese yuan. But none imagines a future in which East Asia remains a zone of competition between China and Japan, or even between China and the United States. They consider the trend toward Chinese regional hegemony unstoppable by any external force.

The Chinese today measure their greatness by the respect their nation is accorded in the international system, by China's new weight in international economic councils, by the solicitousness of other nations and of the world's most powerful multinational corporations. With its seat at the United Nations Security Council and invitations to the G8, China also carries great weight in the diplomatic councils of the world, and even greater weight in its own region, in forums like the East Asian Summit and ASEAN.

But as with all great powers, there is also a military aspect to greatness. The official *Liberation Army Daily* explains, "As China's comprehensive strength is incrementally mounting and her status keeps on going up in international affairs, it is a matter of great importance to strive to construct a military force that is commensurate with China's status and up to the job of defending the interests of China's development, so as to entrench China's international status."[35]

While becoming a great commercial power, China is also becoming a military power. After all, commercial nations are not pacific nations. The United States, Great Britain, Spain, Venice, and ancient Athens all built powerful navies to defend their far-flung commercial interests, and they could pay for those navies with the riches their commerce produced. As China has transformed its economy from the autarky of the Mao years to the present deep entanglement in the international liberal economic order, it, too, has gained a new set of far-flung economic interests. Today China is the world's largest consumer of raw materials, sucking everything from oil and natural gas to wood and metals out of the eager hands of producers and merchants in Asia, the Middle East, Africa, and Latin America. It depends on foreign markets in Europe and the United States that lie across vast oceans. "Never before has China been so closely bound up with the rest of the world as it is today," the authors of China's 2006 Defense White Paper noted.[36] And therefore China needs a modern, capable military.

Since the end of the Cold War, China has been spending increasing amounts of its growing wealth on modernizing and strengthening its military. Although China faces "no tangible or immediate external military threat" and is stronger and more secure in its borders than at any time in the modern era, at present rates of growth—more than 10 percent annually over the past decade—it will soon be spending more on its military than all the nations of the European Union combined.[37] It has shifted its strategic doctrine away from defending the homeland against foreign invasion and toward a strategy of projecting force overseas. Chinese officials speak of extending strategic frontiers progressively outward to what they call the three "island chains": the first, running from Japan to Taiwan to the Philippines; the second, from Sakhalin to the islands of the Southwest Pacific; the third, from the Aleutian Islands off Alaska to the Antarctic.[38] While the

Chinese navy remains far from achieving these more distant ambitions, the Chinese have been steadily replacing their antiquated naval and air forces with modern ships and aircraft, almost all purchased from Russia. Within a few years China will have roughly doubled its fleet of modern submarines and modern guided missile destroyers.[39] For the first time in centuries, China thinks of itself as a sea power.[40]

Behind this shift in strategy is not only an expanding perception of interests but a growing sense of national pride. "Nationalism" is a dirty word in the postmodern Enlightenment lexicon, but there is no shame in a government restoring a nation's honor.[41] Pride in China's growing international status has become one of the great sources of legitimacy of the ruling oligarchy of the Chinese Communist Party. Popular nationalism, sometimes aimed at Japan, sometimes at the United States, grew dramatically in the 1990s. Part of it was due to government education programs designed to bolster the legitimacy of the Communist Party as defender of the Chinese nation. But part of it sprang naturally from the intermingling of historic resentments and a sense of new power. In the mid-1990s, Chinese nationalists expressed their defiance of the West by marching under the banner "China Can Say No." But it is not only fervent nationalists who relish turning the tables on the western great powers; as one Chinese diplomat put it, "Today it is our turn to speak and their turn to listen."[42]

This equation of military strength with international standing and respectability may be troubling to postmodern sensibilities. In Europe, and even in the United States, many believe that military power and nationalism are a deadly combination that should be relegated to the past. China's military buildup has raised concerns and complaints from the United States and China's neighbors, and even in Europe. They have questioned its legitimacy and demanded greater "transparency," insisting that China reveal more candidly the extent and cost of its military programs, as well as their intentions. Lying behind this global complaint about China's military program is the postmodern assumption that an increasingly rich and secure nation like China doesn't need to build up its military capacity or seek self-reliance in preserving access to resources and markets. Western economists puzzle at China's efforts to strike deals with unsavory leaders of oil-producing nations, or to increase its naval capacity to protect the waterways through which its energy supplies pass. Don't the Chinese understand that in the globalized world one can buy oil on the market without cozy relations with the oil despots of the world? Don't they see that the globalized world of international commerce has an interest in keeping waterways open and that China's buildup is therefore unnecessary?

Chinese leaders don't believe any of this, and with reason. Like all rising powers throughout history, like the United States, Japan, and Germany at the end of the nineteenth century, they fear that the rest of the world may conspire against them. Like the Russians, the Chinese believe that to be a great power they must be independent and self-reliant. For decades China, like most other nations in the world, allowed the American navy to be the great protector of its interests abroad, patrolling the sea lanes, guarding the oil supplies, insuring the international free flow of commerce with its battleships and aircraft carriers. The U.S. Navy guards the Malacca Straits, for instance, China's lifeline to Middle East oil. But these days Premier Hu Jintao worries about a "Malacca dilemma." The dilemma is not new. It is the Chinese perception of themselves that is changing as their power grows. As they grow stronger, they worry they will be prevented from fulfilling their ambitions and their destiny, that they will be denied the full extent of the national growth and international standing they believe they need and deserve. And they fear that the frustration of their people's now expansive ambitions could prove to be their downfall.

The Chinese have considered the United States hostile to their ambitions for decades. Long before Europeans began expressing concern about the "hyperpower," long before world opinion complained about America's arrogance and hegemonism, Chinese observers had pointed to its "superhegemonist" ambitions.[43] They knew George H. W. Bush's new world order meant a dominant United States, with Russia and China in distinctly secondary roles. They knew all about the indispensable nation. The American-led condemnation of the Tiananmen Square violence, which resulted in the loss of China's bid for the 2000 Olympics; the confrontation between the United States and China over Taiwan in 1995 and 1996, ending in the dispatch of two American aircraft carrier battle groups to the waters off China; and then the war in Kosovo, which drew Chinese ire even before the U.S. Air Force bombed the Chinese embassy in Belgrade—all these events produced among the Chinese a perception of the United States as "not just arrogant," but as actively seeking "to prevent China from prospering and gaining its rightful place at the top of the world system."[44] The current Chinese prime minister Wen Jiabao believed even before 2001 that the United States was "trying to preserve its status as the world's sole superpower, and will not allow any country the chance to pose a challenge to it."[45] In the last years of Bill Clinton's administration, Chinese strategic thinkers saw not the multipolar world they wanted and expected but a world in which "the superpower is more super, and the many great powers are less great."[46]

It is not surprising that the Chinese tend to dismiss the postmodern view that national power, including military power, is passé. They may speak of transcending traditional geopolitics. They may claim no interest in traditional forms of power. But their actual policy is to accumulate more of it. Nor should anyone blame them for seeing the world as it is. Europeans and Americans may insist that China pursue a different, more "responsible" model of development as a great nation, that it should embrace the era of geo-economics and globalization. But the Chinese might well ask whether the world is really as Europeans imagine it, and whether the United States itself would ever follow its own advice and abjure power politics.

The fact is, Asia is not the European Union, and China is not Luxembourg. China's ambitions, its desire for strategic independence, its growing sense of its own importance, its concern for status and honor, and the military buildup that it is undertaking to establish and defend its new position in the world are the actions not of a postmodern power, or of a status quo power, but of a most traditional and normal rising power.

Every day the Chinese military prepares for a possible war with the United States over Taiwan. It is a war the Chinese government would like very much to avoid but believes may someday be unavoidable. The Chinese leadership, with the support of the Chinese people, insists that Taiwan must eventually be "reunified" with the mainland and that this is a vital national interest. They claim they would prefer to fight a war, including against the powerful United States, rather than permit Taiwan's independence. Therefore, they prepare for it.

Why do the Chinese feel this way? No genuinely postmodern power interested only in "peaceful development" and transcending the traditional path of great powers would stake out such a position. After more than a century of separation, and after decades of de facto Taiwanese independence, the Chinese society, culture, and economy are not suffering for lack of 24 million Taiwanese, the majority of whom do not consider themselves part of China. The two sides engage in billions of dollars' worth of mutually profitable trade and would not engage in appreciably more if Taiwan were suddenly to raise the flag of the Beijing government. China may find Taiwan's aspirations for independence objectionable. But in Europe, all kinds of subnational movements aspire to greater autonomy or even independence from their national governments, and with less justification than Taiwan: the

Catalans in Spain, for instance, or the Flemish in Belgium, or even the Scots in the United Kingdom. No war threatens in Barcelona or Antwerp or Edinburgh.

But the Chinese and Europeans live in different centuries. On the subject of Taiwan, China's is a traditional nineteenth-century mentality. The issue is not only one of material interests. It is a matter of national pride and honor, connected closely to the question of national sovereignty. The Chinese believe they were robbed of that sovereignty in the nineteenth century, and they want it back. Past injustices and offenses need to be corrected so that the nation can move forward to the future with pride and self-confidence. These are not trivial matters. Nations have historically considered honor and pride worth fighting for, often at the sacrifice of economic interests, and disputed territories have often been the cause of war.

What began as China's desire to restore its pride and honor, moreover, has become entangled in the larger question of its regional and historical ambitions. Taiwan's refusal to join the mainland and its persistent efforts to obtain greater international recognition and perhaps even independence is a problem not only because it stands in the way of unification; it is also a rebuke, a humiliating rejection of Beijing's Asian centrality by an undeniably Chinese people. If Taiwan will not accept China's leadership in East Asia, who else can be expected to? By rejecting unification, the Taiwanese make themselves allies of America's determined Asian regional hegemony. To the Chinese, in fact, Taiwan has become the embodiment of

American post–Cold War ideological hostility and strategic opposition. It is a "proxy battlefield" in the Sino-American confrontation.[47]

Americans sometimes feel the same way. When the Clinton administration sent aircraft carriers to the Taiwan Strait in 1996, Clinton's secretary of defense, William Perry, declared, "Beijing should know, and this U.S. fleet will remind them, that while they are a great military power, the strongest, the premier military power in the Western Pacific is the United States."[48]

If East Asia today resembles late-nineteenth- and early-twentieth-century Europe, then Taiwan could be the Sarajevo of the Sino-American confrontation. A comparatively minor incident, a provocative declaration by Taiwan's president or a resolution passed by its legislature, could infuriate the Chinese and lead them to choose war, despite their reluctance. It would be comforting to imagine that this will all dissipate as China grows richer and more confident, but history suggests that as China grows more confident it will grow less, not more, tolerant of the obstacles in its path. The Chinese themselves have few illusions on this score. They believe this great strategic rivalry will only "increase with the ascension of Chinese power."[49]

JAPAN: A RETURN TO NORMALCY

CHINA AND THE UNITED STATES ARE NOT the only actors on the Asian scene. China is not the only Asian great power with ambitions and aspirations for greater global influence and stature. There is Japan, and there is India. The other great fault line of the new geopolitics runs along an arc from Northeast Asia through the Southeast and into Central Asia, where the interests and ambitions of China, Japan, India, Russia, and the United States all overlap and collide.

It is easy to forget, as everyone concentrates on China's rise as a great power, that Japan is a great power, too. Its economy remains the second largest in the world, a remarkable fact given its relatively small population, smaller territory, and lack of natural resources. Meanwhile, the Japanese military is one of the world's most modern. Although Japan spends barely more than 1 percent of its national wealth on defense, that amounts to $40 billion a year, among the three or four highest defense budgets in the world. And while Japan is not a nuclear power, and does not want to become one, in a crisis it could build a potent nuclear arsenal quickly.[50]

Japan is not only a genuine great power but increasingly displays great power ambitions. The shift has been most marked since the end of the Cold War. Many Japanese thinkers and policymakers initially shared the general optimism about the nature of the international system after the Cold War. But that optimism faded faster in Asia than it did in Europe. A growing perception of danger from China and North Korea convinced Japanese leaders and much of the Japanese public that Northeast Asia remained a world where power politics still mattered and war was still possible.[51] Since the mid-1990s, Japan has upgraded its Defense Ministry's status, increased (albeit marginally) the percentage of money spent on defense, strengthened its security relationship with the United States, expanded Japan's global military role to include peacekeeping, offered Japanese assistance in Iraq and Afghanistan, and generally taken a more expansive view of the role of Japanese power in the world.

Although Japanese politics has been volatile, "it is not difficult to discern the nationalistic impulse here today," as one observer of Japanese society has noted. "It is found in comics and movies, in an enthusiasm for World Cup soccer, in an indignation over North Korean missiles and, far from least, in Japan's anxiety over China's emerging influence." Nor should anyone imagine that Japanese prosperity is the antidote, any more than it has been for China or Russia. "Japan has been searching to discover its genuine identity," observes veteran politician Koichi Kato. "For decades we thought this lay in economic achievement— in catching up to America. But we've done that now. We're affluent. So for the past 20 years we've been soul-searching—looking for something we should aspire to next."[52] Being relegated to second-class status by a rising China is not among those aspirations.

Rivalry between Japan and China is one of the enduring features of the global landscape, stretching back to the end of the nineteenth century and for many centuries before that. For more than a thousand years, the Chinese looked down on the Japanese as an inferior race within their Sino-centric universe. They treated Japan either "benevolently as a student or younger brother" or malevolently as a nation of pirates, but China's superiority and

Japan's inferiority were part of the natural order of things and the only basis for truly "harmonious" relations.[53]

Then, at the end of the nineteenth century, a rising, westernizing Japan—"rich nation, strong army"—thrashed China in the war of 1895. Chinese scholars still call it the greatest humiliation in their nation's long history. During the era of Japanese domination that followed, China suffered not only humiliation but aggression of an especially brutal nature, epitomized by the horrors perpetrated in Nanjing in the 1930s. Those kinds of memories die hard.[54] When the Chinese people sing their national anthem—"Arise, Ye who refuse to be slaves! ... Millions of hearts with one mind.... Everybody must roar his defiance!"—they are singing about a Japanese invasion that elderly Chinese can still recall and every Chinese child learns about in school. Putting Japan back in its place, restoring the harmonious order of Chinese superiority, as well as Japanese acceptance of that superiority, is a potent if unspoken Chinese ambition.

The Japanese are no fonder of the Chinese than the Chinese are of them. They do not relish the role of little brother. They are aware that China uses memories of World War II to try to isolate Japan from the rest of Asia. That is one reason, though not the only reason, that Japanese prime ministers have until recently been defiantly visiting the Yasukuni Shrine, where Japanese war criminals are honored. Japanese leaders are reluctant to bow to Chinese demands at a time when signs of growing Chinese power and hegemonism seem to them unmistakable. The Chinese military buildup that began in the 1990s, Chinese nuclear tests in 1995 and 1996, the ballistic missiles fired off Taiwan's coast, Chinese territorial claims in the East and South China Seas—all have had their effect on Japanese public opinion. Perceptions that the balance of power may be shifting away from Japan and toward China have certainly helped fuel Japanese nationalism, as well as Japanese efforts to counter the trend by drawing closer to the United States and other powers in Asia.

These deep ruts worn by centuries of conflict have not been washed away by two decades of trade and globalization. China has become Japan's largest trading partner, four million tourists and businessmen travel between the two countries every year, and Mandarin has become the second most popular foreign language studied in Japan, after English.[55] Yet hostility between the two peoples continues to broaden and deepen.[56] Between 1988 and 2004, the percentage of Japanese with positive feelings toward China declined from 69 percent to 38 percent.[57]

The competition between China and Japan remains a central feature of Asian geopolitics. Both seek to augment their status and power relative to the other, in the military and strategic as well as economic and political realms. Chinese diplomats work to prevent Japan from gaining a seat as permanent member on the United Nations Security Council. Japanese foreign policy has aimed at warmer relations with Taiwan. Were China to take military action against Taiwan, the Japanese would view it as a serious risk to their nation's security. Both nations compete for friends and allies, in Southeast Asia, South Asia, and Europe. Both try to outmaneuver each other in diplomatic forums. And both seek to cement military relationships with other Asian states.

INDIA AND THE
ARGUMENT OF POWER

IN ASIA, HOWEVER, it is a three-way, not a two-way, competition. India is a third ambitious great power, the hegemon of the Asian subcontinent. It is also another striking example of how easily commerce and globalization can contribute to, rather than diminish, a nation's great power ambitions. A prime example of success in Thomas Friedman's "flat" world, with growth rates approaching those of China in recent years, India's dynamic services and high-technology industries are uniquely suited to thrive in a globalized age. Yet India is not some disembodied call center suspended in the global ether. It is a nation of flesh and blood, with all the passions, resentments, and ambitions of the human soul. The same economic dynamism and plunge into global commercial competition that brought India out of its shell economically have also brought it out of its shell geopolitically.

Like China, India has a proud history of regional primacy, a deep resentment at its long colonial subjugation to a European power, a sense of manifest destiny, and a belief in its impending greatness on the world stage. The sense of its own greatness is not new, but it has changed with the times. In the years after independence, India conceived of itself not as a traditional great power but as a great moral counterweight to the imperial powers and superpowers of the twentieth century. As C. Raja Mohan explains, India's leaders expressed contempt for "power politics" and saw their nation's emergence on the world scene "as the harbinger of a new set of principles of peaceful coexistence and multilateralism which if applied properly would transform the world"—a European-style worldview before Europeans themselves had adopted it.[58]

The rapid economic growth of the 1990s, however, has given Indians a different picture of themselves as a great power, not in a postmodern but in a traditional geopolitical sense. As Mohan notes, "While independent India always had a sense of its own greatness," the possibility of becoming a great power in its own right "never seemed realistic until the Indian economy began to grow rapidly in the 1990s." With growing power came a growing belief in power. Like the Chinese, Japanese, and Russians, the Indians realized that the post–Cold War world was not to be a postmodern paradise after all, and that power politics still dominated international relations. Since 1991, India has moved from emphasizing the "power of the argument" to a new stress on the "argument of power."[59]

Nothing epitomized this drive to power more than India's single-minded determination to become recognized and accepted as a nuclear weapons state. Economic success played a critical role here, for when Indian leaders decided to make the fateful decision to conduct a series of nuclear tests in 1998, the economic growth of the previous decade gave them the self-confidence to believe that the world would not punish such a valuable part of the global economy for long. India's nuclear ambitions have their basis in strategic concerns about possible conflicts with Pakistan and its Chinese patron. But they have also been a matter of honor, status, and self-respect. Can a nation consider itself a great power in the modern world if it is not also a member of the nuclear club? Ask France, Great Britain, China, or Iran.

So now, as the scholar Sunil Khilnani sardonically observes, Indians "have become enamoured of the idea that we are soon to become a permanent invitee to the perpetual soiree of great powers, and so must dust ourselves off and dress for the part." But what, he asks, should India's role be?[60] Like Russia and China, India sees its geopolitical interests in concentric circles of power and influence emanating outward. In its immediate neighborhood it seeks primacy, a kind of benevolent hegemony, exercising predominant influence over smaller neighbors such as Nepal, Sri Lanka, and the major islands of the Indian Ocean while excluding other great powers, principally China, from establishing relationships with those smaller states on India's periphery. In its "extended neighborhood," which includes the Indian Ocean and its vast littoral, it has sought to preserve a favorable power balance and to prevent others, again principally China, from making gains at its expense. Finally, in the world at large, it has sought to play, at the very least, the role of "swing state in the global balance of power."[61] As Mohan put it, "India's new economic and foreign policies have given India a real opportunity to realize the vision of Lord Curzon, the British viceroy at the turn of the twentieth century, of Indian leadership in the region stretching from Aden to Malacca."[62]

Like all rising and ambitious powers, India faces obstacles, and the biggest, in the view of many Indians, is

China. When India conducted its nuclear weapons tests in 1998, its prime minister cited the threat from China, the "nuclear weapons state on our borders, a state which committed armed aggression against India in 1962" and which "has materially helped another neighbor of ours"—Pakistan—"to become a covert nuclear weapons state."[63] The Indian defense minister bluntly called China "India's threat number one."[64] India has since sought to temper its rhetoric and pursue better relations with China, but the strategic competition between the two great powers endures. There are some old unsettled border disputes, and China's support of Pakistan still rankles. But the great power jostling has also taken new forms.

Indian defense officials complain of China's "growing naval expansion in the Indian Ocean Region," and its growing "military and maritime links with countries like Myanmar, Bangladesh, Sri Lanka, Maldives, Seychelles, Mauritius and Madagascar." A visit by Chinese premier Hu Jintao to Seychelles this past year provoked an official rebuke from India's foreign minister, who asserted his country's "strong stake in the security and stability of these waters."[65] Indian strategists see China funding Burma's navy to India's east, and to India's west, China is investing in construction of a deep-sea port on Pakistan's coast, near the entrance to the Persian Gulf. The Chinese, meanwhile, see India working to develop close military ties to the nations of Southeast Asia, which Beijing regards as within its own sphere of influence. Chinese strategists view India warily as "a non–status quo power . . . deeply dissatisfied with its current international status" and with evident "great power ambitions."[66] Both see themselves as natural leaders in their parts of Asia, but increasingly their spheres intersect and overlap, and neither is willing to give way.[67]

War between them seems about as unlikely as it ever has been—which is to say it is not unthinkable. But even without any immediate prospect of conflict, their geo-political competition is reshaping the patterns of international affairs. As in the nineteenth and early twentieth centuries, the great powers are forming combinations, formal and informal alliances, to protect their interests and further their ambitions. China has its alliance with Pakistan. India, in turn, is developing closer ties to Japan, as well as to the United States. When China tried to exclude India from the first East Asian summit in December 2005, Japan took India's side. When Pakistan offered China observer status in the South Asian Association for Regional Cooperation, India brought in Japan, South Korea, and the United States to counterbalance Beijing's influence.[68] Japan, meanwhile, has made India a partner in its strategy in Asia, steering investment and development assistance India's way and engaging in military cooperation, especially in the Indian Ocean. When the Japanese and Indian prime ministers met last year in New Delhi, they agreed that "a strong, prosperous and dynamic India is in the interest of Japan and a strong, prosperous and dynamic Japan is in the interest of India."[69]

These are new developments in the Asian balance of power, and the shifting combinations increasingly have a military dimension. In the summer of 2007, a massive naval exercise was held in the Bay of Bengal, a critical stretch of water close to both the Malacca Straits and Burma. The participants included the United States, with two aircraft carrier battle groups, as well as India, Japan, Australia, and Singapore. It was the first time these nations, whose geographical positions stretch all along China's periphery, from the northeast to the southwest, had come together in this manner. China duly protested to each nation that participated and was duly assured that the exercises had nothing to do with the containment of any power. But the exercises were a symbol of the new fragmenting world and a harbinger of things to come.

Another harbinger was the unprecedented land battle exercises conducted at the same time in Russia, in which thousands of Chinese and Russian forces joined together with those of five Central Asian nations. The exercises followed on the heels of a meeting of the Shanghai Co-operation Organization and its invited guest, President Mahmoud Ahmadinejad of Iran.

IRAN AND REGIONAL HEGEMONY

IRAN, TOO, fits the old model of national ambition. A proud and ancient civilization, Persian Iran is famous in its region for a sense of superiority, even arrogance, and a belief in its own destiny. Like China, India, and now Russia, Iran also has a historical sense of grievance. Once the great superpower of its world, Iran spent much of the last two centuries plundered, colonized, and humiliated by the European empires. As a Shi'a nation in a region dominated by Sunni Arab governments, it has also felt under siege theologically. It is hardly surprising that Iran should desire to break out and assert itself, both out of calculation of interest and out of a desire for honor and respect. As Ray Takeyh observes, Iran believes that by "virtue of its size and historical achievements," it has "the right to emerge as the local hegemon" in the Middle East and Persian Gulf. The only questions today are "how it should consolidate its sphere of influence and whether it can emerge as a regional hegemon in defiance of or accommodation with the United States."[70]

So far, the choice has been defiance. As more than one Iranian leader has made clear, Iran defines and ennobles itself by its willingness to stand up to the United States, the predominant and overbearing superpower, which also happens to be the Great Satan. These passions and ambitions long preceded the Bush administration, as did Iran's conviction that only as a nuclear weapons state could it fend off pressures from the American superpower and its allies. It learned this lesson not from the Iraq War of 2003 but from the Iraq War of 1991, when the United States demonstrated how easily it could brush aside even the massive Iraqi conventional army that Iran itself had been unable to defeat. But Iran's nuclear program is not only about security. Like India, Iran pursues nuclear weapons to establish itself as a great power in its region and beyond. Because the western liberal world insists on denying Iran its "right" to nuclear power, the question has also become a matter of honor.

The notion that the present Iranian regime would

trade away its honor and self-respect, indeed its very sense of itself, in return for material goods such as money or unreliable security guarantees from the Great Satan seems fanciful. Instead, like the other ambitious powers jostling for position in the world, Iran looks for partners with shared interests, or at least shared opponents. It does not find them in the West, but in the East. As top Iranian official Ali Larijani points out, "There are big states in the Eastern Hemisphere such as Russia, China and India. These states can play a balancing role in today's world."[71]

Iran, with its unique brand of national ambition, hardly speaks for all of the Muslim world. Nor does Osama bin Laden. Islam is too diverse, not only because of sectarian differences but because of the many different contours of a Muslim world that stretches from Indonesia to Morocco. Yet the mullahs and Al Qaeda, as well as groups such as Hamas, Hezbollah, and the Muslim Brotherhood, do reflect genuine feelings in the Muslim world that are not so unlike the nationalist resentments of Russians, Chinese, and Indians. Like national movements elsewhere, Islamists have a yearning for respect, including self-respect, and a desire for honor. Their identity has been molded partly in defiance against stronger and often oppressive outside powers, and also by memories of ancient superiority over those same powers. China had its "century of humiliation." Islamists have more than a century of humiliation to look back on, a humiliation of which Israel has become the living symbol. This is partly why even Muslims who are neither radical nor fundamentalist sometimes offer their sympathy and even their support to violent extremists who can turn the tables on the dominant liberal West, and particularly on a dominant America, which implanted and still feeds the Israeli cancer in their midst.

THE AMBITIOUS SUPERPOWER

AND WHAT ABOUT THE UNITED STATES? Is America's special kind of nationalism and ambition, with its sense of a universal mission and belief in the righteousness of its own power, any less potent today than over the past two centuries? Did the end of the Cold War change the United States, soften its manners, relax its grip on international power? When the Soviet Union and its empire collapsed, did the United States pull back from its extended global involvements and become a more passive, restrained presence in the world?

The answer to these questions is no. When the Cold War ended, the United States pressed forward. Under the administrations of the first President Bush and Bill Clinton, it extended and strengthened its alliances. It began exerting influence in places like Central Asia and the Caucasus, which most Americans did not even know existed before 1989. American power, unchecked by Soviet power, filled vacuums and attempted to establish, where possible, the kind of democratic and free-market capitalist order that Americans preferred. Although the rate of increase in defense spending declined marginally during the 1990s, the technological advances in American weaponry far outstripped the rest of the world and placed the United States more than ever in a special category of military superpower. The natural result was a greater proclivity to employ this force for a wide range of purposes, from humanitarian intervention in Somalia and Kosovo to regime change in Panama and Iraq. Between 1989 and 2001, the United States intervened with force in foreign lands more frequently than at any other time in its history—an average of one significant new military action every sixteen months—and far more than any other power in the same stretch of time.[72]

This expansive, even aggressive global policy was consistent with American foreign policy traditions. Americans' sense of themselves, the essence of their patriotism, has been inextricably tied to a belief in their nation's historic global significance. Inspired by this perception of the world and themselves, they have amassed power and influence and deployed them in ever widening arcs around the globe on behalf of interests, ideals, and ambitions, both tangible and intangible. As a matter of global strategy, they have preferred a "preponderance of power" to a balance of power with other nations.[73] They have insisted on preserving and if possible extending regional predominance in East Asia; the Middle East; the Western Hemisphere; until recently, Europe; and now, increasingly, Central Asia. They have attempted to carry out changes of regime when they deemed them useful to advance American ideals or American interests.[74] They have ignored the United Nations, their allies, and international law when these institutions and rules became obstacles to their objectives.[75] They have been impatient with the status quo and seen America as a catalyst for change in human affairs. As former French foreign minister Hubert Védrine once observed (during the Clinton years), most "great American leaders and thinkers have never doubted for an instant that the United States was chosen by providence as the 'indispensable nation' and that it must remain dominant for the sake of humankind."[76]

Since World War II, when, as Americans see it, the United States rushed into the breach to save the world from self-destruction, a guiding principle of American foreign policy has been that no one else can quite be trusted to keep the world safe for democratic principles— not America's enemies, certainly, but not its allies, either. "We stand tall and we see further than other countries into the future," Secretary of State Madeleine Albright remarked in 1998.[77]

The paradox is that most Americans do not believe they have any national ambitions at all beyond basic security and economic well-being. Much less do they believe they seek global primacy. Americans consider themselves by nature an inward-looking and insular people, always just a step away from retreating into their fortress—even as, decade after decade after decade, they deploy troops in dozens of countries around the world and use their great economic, political, and cultural power to influence the behavior of millions, even billions of people in other lands every day. In the popular imagination, and even in the reckoning of the elite foreign policy establishment, the United States is at most a "Reluctant Sheriff," with its boots up on the desk, minding its own business until the next gang of outlaws rides into town.[78] It is as if the United States somehow arrived at the present unprecedented pinnacle of global power by accident, that Americans neither desire nor enjoy their role as the world's predominant power.

The truth is they both desire it and rue it. Americans want what they want, and not just economic opportunity and security but also a world that roughly suits their political and moral preferences. They would naturally prefer not to pay a high price for such a world, however, and it is not only the financial price Americans would like to avoid, or even the cost in lives. It is also the moral price, the ethical burdens of power. Americans' deeply rooted republicanism has always made them suspicious of power, even their own. But in shaping a world to suit their values, they have compelled others to bend to their will, sometimes by force, sometimes by softer but no less persuasive means. A nation that cherishes self-determination is uncomfortable depriving others of that right, even in a good cause. This problem is not unique to the United States. The great moral conundrum of humanity, much commented upon by Reinhold Niebuhr and other realists of the brutal mid-twentieth century, is that moral ends often cannot be achieved without recourse to actions that by themselves seem of dubious morality. "We take, and must continue to take, morally hazardous actions to preserve our civilization." To be virtuous is not to be innocent.[79]

In theory Americans could give up trying to shape the world around them. In practice they have never for a moment ceased to do so, not even during their brief periods of supposed isolationism. Instead they have continually searched for a way to reconcile their demand for a certain kind of world and their wish to avoid the costs, including the moral costs, of imposing that world on others.

That was why many Americans of all political stripes seized so eagerly on the new world order. It was the great escape. For conservatives, the Cold War had been about the ideological struggle against communism.[80] When communism collapsed, Jeane Kirkpatrick spoke for a majority of conservatives, and perhaps many liberals, as well, when she hoped the United States could cease carrying the "unusual burdens" of global leadership that it had borne so "heroically" during the Cold War and finally become a "normal nation."[81] For many other American liberals, the hope was somewhat different. As the world embraced democratic values, the United States could help build the kind of international order imagined by Woodrow Wilson, a world of law and institutions that would uphold democratic principles and defend morality and justice without requiring the constant, morally dubious exercise of American power. If American power had to be employed, it would be as the indispensable nation acting in service to the international community.

THE AXIS OF DEMOCRACY AND THE ASSOCIATION OF AUTOCRATS

LIKE THE EXPECTATIONS of an end to great power competition, however, these hopes for an ideological "end of history" were based on a set of historical circumstances that proved fleeting. Communism passed from the scene, but powerful challengers to democracy have not.

Since the mid-1990s, the nascent democratic transformation in Russia has given way to what may best be described as a "czarist" political system, in which all important decisions are taken by one man and his powerful coterie.[82] Vladimir Putin and his spokesmen speak of "democracy," but they define the term much as the Chinese do. For Putin, democracy is not so much about competitive elections as about the implementation of the popular will. The regime is democratic because the government consults with and listens to the Russian people, discerns what they need and want, and then attempts to give it to them. As Ivan Krastev notes, "The Kremlin thinks not in terms of citizens' rights but in terms of the population's needs."[83] Elections do not offer a choice but only a chance to ratify choices made by Putin. He controls all institutions of the federal government, from the cabinet to the legislature. The legal system is a tool to be used against political opponents. The party system has been purged of political groups not approved by Putin. The power apparatus around Putin controls most of the national media, especially television.[84]

A majority of Russians seem content with autocratic rule, at least for now. Unlike communism, Putin's rule does not impinge much on their personal lives if they stay out of politics. Unlike their experience with the tumultuous Russian democracy of the 1990s, the present government, thanks to the high prices of oil and gas, has at least produced a rising standard of living. Putin's efforts to undo the humiliating post–Cold War settlement and restore the greatness of Russia is popular. His political advisors believe that "avenging the demise of the Soviet Union will keep us in power."[85]

For Putin, there is a symbiosis between the nature of his rule and his success in returning Russia to great power status. Strength and control at home allow Russia to be strong abroad. Strength abroad justifies strong rule at home. Russia's growing international clout also shields Putin's autocracy from foreign pressures. European and American statesmen find they have a full plate of international issues on which a strong Russia can make life easier or harder, from energy supplies to Iran. Under the circumstances, they are far less eager to confront the Russian government over the fairness of its elections or the openness of its political system.

Putin has created a guiding national philosophy out of the correlation between power abroad and autocracy at home. He calls Russia a "sovereign democracy," a term that neatly encapsulates Russia's return to greatness, its escape from the impositions of the West, and its adoption of an "eastern" model of democracy. In Putin's view, only a great and powerful Russia is strong enough to defend and advance its interests, and also strong enough to resist foreign demands for western political reforms that Russia neither needs nor wants.[86] In the 1990s, Russia wielded little influence on the world stage but opened itself wide to the intrusions of foreign businessmen and foreign governments. Putin wants Russia to have great influence over others around the world while shielding itself from the influence of unwelcome global forces.[87]

Putin looks to China as a model, and for good reason. While the Soviet Union collapsed and lost everything after 1989, as first Mikhail Gorbachev and then Boris Yeltsin sued for peace with the West and invited its meddling, Chinese leaders weathered their crisis by defying the West. They cracked down at home and then battened down the hatches until the storm of western disapproval blew over. The results in the two great powers were instructive. Russia by the end of the 1990s was flat on its back. China was on its way to unprecedented economic growth, military power, and international influence.

The Chinese learned from the Soviet experience, too. While the democratic world waited after Tiananmen Square for China to resume its inevitable course upward toward liberal democratic modernity, the Chinese Communist Party leadership set about shoring up its dominance in the nation. In recent years, despite repeated predictions in the West of an imminent political opening, the trend has been toward consolidation rather than reform of the Chinese autocracy. As it became clear that the Chinese leadership had no intention of reforming itself out of power, western observers hoped that they might be forced to reform despite themselves, if only to keep China on a path of economic growth and to manage the myriad internal problems that growth brings. But that now seems unlikely, as well. Today, most economists believe China's remarkable growth should be sustainable for some time to come. Keen observers of the Chinese political system see a sufficient combination of competence and ruthlessness on the part of the Chinese leadership to handle problems as they arise, and a populace prepared to accept autocratic government so long as economic growth continues. As scholars Andrew Nathan and Bruce Gilley have written, the present leadership is unlikely to "succumb to a rising tide of problems or surrender graciously to liberal values infiltrated by means of economic globalization." Until events "justify taking a different attitude, the outside world would be well advised to treat the new Chinese leaders as if they are here to stay."[88]

Growing national wealth and autocracy have proven compatible, after all. Autocrats learn and adjust. The autocracies of Russia and China have figured out how to permit open economic activity while suppressing political activity. They have seen that people making money will keep their noses out of politics, especially if they know their noses will be cut off. New wealth gives autocracies a greater ability to control information—to monopolize television stations and to keep a grip on Internet traffic, for instance—often with the assistance of foreign corporations eager to do business with them.[89]

In the long run, rising prosperity may well produce political liberalism, but how long is the long run? It may be too long to have any strategic or geopolitical relevance. As the old joke goes, Germany launched itself on a trajectory of economic modernization in the late nineteenth century and within six decades became a fully fledged democracy. The only problem was what happened in the intervening years. So the world waits for change, but in the meantime two of the world's largest nations, with more than a billion and a half people and the second- and third-largest militaries between them, now have governments committed to autocratic rule and may be able to sustain themselves in power for the foreseeable future.

The power and durability of these autocracies will shape the international system in profound ways. The world is not about to embark on a new ideological struggle of the kind that dominated the Cold War. But the new era, rather than being a time of "universal values," will be one of growing tensions and sometimes confrontation between the forces of democracy and the forces of autocracy.

During the Cold War, it was easy to forget that the struggle between liberalism and autocracy has endured since the Enlightenment. It was the issue that divided the United States from much of Europe in the late eighteenth and early nineteenth centuries. It divided Europe itself through much of the nineteenth century and into the twentieth. Now it is returning to dominate the geopolitics of the twenty-first century.

The presumption over the past decade has been that when Chinese and Russian leaders stopped believing in communism, they stopped believing in anything. They had become pragmatists, without ideology or belief, simply pursuing their own and their nation's interests. But the rulers of China and Russia, like the rulers of autocracies in the past, do have a set of beliefs that guides them in both domestic and foreign policy. It is not an all-encompassing, systematic worldview like Marxism or liberalism. But it is a comprehensive set of beliefs about government and society and the proper relationship between rulers and their people.

The rulers of Russia and China believe in the virtues of a strong central government and disdain the weaknesses of the democratic system. They believe their large and fractious nations need order and stability in order to prosper. They believe that the vacillations and chaos of democracy would impoverish and shatter their nations, and in the case of Russia already did so. They believe that strong rule at home is necessary if their nations are to be strong and respected in the world, capable of safeguarding and advancing their interests. Chinese rulers know from their nation's long and often turbulent history that political disruptions and divisions at home invite foreign interference and depredation. What the world applauded as a political opening in 1989, Chinese leaders regard as a near fatal display of disagreement.

Chinese and Russian leaders are not just autocrats, therefore. They believe in autocracy. The modern liberal mind at "the end of history" may not appreciate the enduring appeal of autocracy in this globalized world. Historically speaking, Russian and Chinese rulers are in illustrious company. The European monarchs of the seventeenth, eighteenth, and nineteenth centuries were thoroughly convinced of the superiority of their form of government. Along with Plato and Aristotle and every other great thinker prior to the eighteenth century, they regarded democracy as the rule of the licentious, greedy, and ignorant mob. In the first half of the twentieth century, for every democratic power like the United States, Great Britain, and France, there was an equally strong autocratic power, in Germany, Russia, and Japan. The many smaller nations around the world were at least as likely to model themselves after the autocracies as the democracies. Only in the past half century has democracy gained widespread popularity around the world, and really only since the 1980s has it become the most common form of government. The rulers of Russia and China are not the first to suggest that it may not be the best.

It is often suggested that the autocrats in Moscow and Beijing are interested only in lining their pockets, that the Chinese leaders are just kleptocrats and that the Kremlin is "Russia, Inc." Of course the rulers of China and Russia look out for themselves, enjoying power for its own sake and also for the wealth and luxuries it brings. But so did many great kings, emperors, and popes of past centuries. People who wield power like wielding power, and it usually makes them rich. But they also believe they wield it in the service of a higher cause. By providing order, by producing economic success, by holding their nations together and leading them to a position of international influence, respectability, and power, they believe they are serving their people. Nor is it at all clear, for the moment, that the majority of people they rule in either China or Russia disagree.

If autocracies have their own set of beliefs, they also have their own set of interests. The rulers of China and Russia may indeed be pragmatic, but they are pragmatic in pursuing policies that will keep themselves in power. Putin sees no distinction between his own interests and Russia's interests. When Louis XIV remarked, *"L'Etat c'est moi,"* he was declaring himself the living embodiment of the French nation, asserting that his interests and France's interests were the same. When Putin declares that he has a "moral right" to continue to rule Russia, he is saying that it is in Russia's interest for him to remain in power. And just as Louis XIV could not imagine it being in the interests of France for the monarchy to perish, neither can Putin imagine it could be in Russia's interest for him to give up power. As China scholar Minxin Pei has pointed out, when Chinese leaders face the choice between economic efficiency and the preservation of power, they choose power.[90] That is their pragmatism.

The autocrats' interest in self-preservation affects their approach to foreign policy, as well. In the age of monarchy, foreign policy served the interests of the monarch. In the age of religious conflict, it served the interests of the church. In the modern era, democracies have pursued foreign policies to make the world safer for democracy. Today the autocrats pursue foreign policies aimed at making the world safe, if not for all autocracies, then at least for their own.

Russia is a prime example of how a nation's governance at home shapes its relations with the rest of the world. A democratizing Russia, and even Gorbachev's democratizing Soviet Union, took a fairly benign view of NATO and tended to have good relations with neighbors that were treading the same path toward democracy. But today Putin regards NATO as a hostile entity, calls its enlargement "a serious provocation," and asks "against whom is this expansion intended?"[91] Yet NATO is no more aggressive or provocative toward Moscow today than it was in Gorbachev's time. If anything, it is less so. NATO has become more benign, just as Russia has become more aggressive. When Russia was more democratic, Russian leaders saw their interests as intimately bound up with the liberal democratic world. Today the Russian government is suspicious of the democracies, especially those near its borders.[92]

This is understandable. For all their growing wealth and influence, the twenty-first-century autocracies remain a minority in the world. As Chinese scholars put it, democratic liberalism became dominant after the fall of Soviet communism and is sustained by an "international hierarchy dominated by the United States and its democratic allies," a "U.S.-centered great power group." The Chinese and Russians feel like an "outlier" from this exclusive and powerful clique.[93] As one official complained at Davos this year, "You western countries, you decide the rules, you give the grades, you say, 'You have been a bad boy.'"[94] As Putin wryly complains, "We are constantly being taught about democracy."[95]

The post–Cold War world looks very different when seen from autocratic Beijing and Moscow than it does from democratic Washington, London, Paris, Berlin, or Brussels. For the leaders in Beijing, it was not so long ago that the international democratic community, led by the United States, turned on China with a rare unity, imposing economic sanctions and even more painful diplomatic isolation after the crackdown at Tiananmen Square. The Chinese Communist Party has had a "persisting sense of insecurity ever since," a "constant fear of being singled out and targeted by the leading powers, especially the United States," and a "profound concern for the regime's survival, bordering on a sense of being under siege."[96]

In the 1990s, the democratic world, led by the United States, toppled autocratic governments in Panama and Haiti and twice made war against Slobodan Milosevic's Serbia. International nongovernmental organizations (NGOs), well funded by western governments, trained opposition parties and supported electoral reforms in Central and Eastern Europe and in Central Asia. In 2000, internationally financed opposition forces and international election monitors finally brought down Milosevic. Within a year he was shipped off to The Hague and five years later was dead in prison.

From 2003 to 2005, western democratic countries and NGOs provided pro-western and pro-democratic parties and politicians with the financing and organizational help that allowed them to topple other autocrats in Georgia, Kyrgyzstan, Ukraine, and Lebanon. Europeans and Americans celebrated these revolutions and saw in them the natural unfolding of humanity's destined political evolution toward liberal democracy. But leaders in Beijing and Moscow saw these events in geopolitical terms, as western-funded, CIA-inspired coups that furthered the hegemony of America and its European allies. The upheavals in Ukraine and Georgia, Dmitri Trenin notes, "further poisoned the Russian-Western relationship" and helped persuade the Kremlin to "complete its turnaround in foreign policy."[97]

The color revolutions worried Putin not only because they checked his regional ambitions but also because he feared that the examples of Ukraine and Georgia could be repeated in Russia. They convinced him by 2006 to control, restrict, and in some cases close down the activities of international NGOs. Even today he warns against the "jackals" in Russia who "got a crash course from foreign experts, got trained in neighboring republics and will try here now."[98]

His worries may seem absurd, or disingenuous, but they are not misplaced. In the post–Cold War era, a triumphant liberalism has sought to expand its triumph by establishing as an international principle the right of the "international community" to intervene against sovereign states that abuse the rights of their people. International NGOs interfere in domestic politics; international organizations like the Organization for Security and Cooperation in Europe monitor and pass judgment on elections; international legal experts talk about modifying international law to include such novel concepts as "the responsibility to protect" or a "voluntary sovereignty waiver." In theory, these innovations apply to everyone. In practice, they chiefly provide democratic nations the right to intervene in the affairs of nondemocratic nations. Unfortunately for the Chinese, Russians, and other autocracies, this is one area where there is no great transatlantic divide. The United States, though traditionally jealous of its own sovereignty, has always been ready to interfere in the internal affairs of other nations. The nations of Europe, once the great proponents (in theory) of the Westphalian order of inviolable state sovereignty, have now reversed course and produced a system, as Robert Cooper puts it, of constant "mutual interference in each other's domestic affairs, right down to beer and sausages."[99]

This has become one of the great schisms in the international system dividing the democratic world and the autocracies. For three centuries, international law, with its strictures against interference in the internal affairs of nations, has tended to protect autocracies. Now the democratic world is in the process of removing that protection, while the autocrats rush to defend the principle of sovereign inviolability.

The war in Kosovo in 1999 was a more dramatic and disturbing turning point for Russia and China than was the Iraq War of 2003. Both nations opposed NATO's intervention, and not only because China's embassy was bombed by an American warplane and Russia's distant Slavic cousins in Serbia were on the receiving end of the NATO air campaign. When Russia threatened to block military action at the United Nations Security Council, NATO simply sidestepped the United Nations and took it upon itself to authorize action, thus negating one of Russia's few tools of international influence. From Moscow's perspective, it was a clear violation of international law, not only because the war lacked a UN imprimatur but because it was an intervention into a sovereign nation that had committed no external aggression. The "interventionist emphasis on human rights," according to the Chinese, was only a new and potent strategy of global domination by "liberal hegemonism."[100] Years later, Putin was still insisting that the western nations "leave behind this disdain for international law" and not attempt to "substitute NATO or the EU for the UN."[101]

The Russians and Chinese were in good company. At the time, no less an authority than Henry Kissinger warned that "the abrupt abandonment of the concept of national sovereignty" risked a world unmoored from any notion of international legal order. The United States, of course, paid this little heed—it had intervened and over-thrown sovereign governments dozens of times through-out its history. But even postmodern Europe set aside legal niceties in the interest of what it regarded as a higher Enlightenment morality. As Robert Cooper has observed, Europe was driven to act by "the collective memory of the holocaust and the streams of displaced people created by extreme nationalism in the Second World War." This "common historical experience" provided all the justifica-tion necessary. Kissinger warned that in a world of "com-peting truths," such a doctrine risked chaos. Cooper responded that postmodern Europe was "no longer a zone of competing truths."[102]

But the conflict between international law and liberal morality is one the democracies have not been able to finesse. As Chinese officials asked at the time of Tianan-men Square and have continued to ask, "What right does the U.S. government have to . . . flagrantly interfere in China's internal affairs?"[103] What right, indeed? Only the liberal creed grants the right, the belief that all men are created equal and have certain inalienable rights that must not be abridged by governments, that governments derive their power and legitimacy only from the consent of the governed and have a duty to protect their citizens' right to life, liberty, and property. To those who share this liberal faith, foreign policies and even wars that defend these principles, as in Kosovo, can be right even if established international law says they are wrong. But to the Chinese, the Russians, and others who don't share this worldview, the United States and its democratic allies succeed in imposing their views on others not because they are right but only because they are powerful enough to do so. To nonliberals, the international liberal order is not progress. It is oppression.

This is more than a dispute over theory and the niceties of international jurisprudence. It concerns the fundamental legitimacy of governments, which for autocrats can be a matter of life and death. China's rulers haven't forgotten that if the democratic world had had its way in 1989, they would now be out of office, possibly imprisoned, or worse. Putin complains that "we are seeing a greater and greater disdain for the basic principles of international law," and he does not just mean the illegal use of force but also the imposition of "economic, political, cultural and educational policies." He decries the way "independent legal norms" are being reshaped to conform to "one state's legal system," that of the western democracies, and the way international institutions like the Organization for Security and Cooperation in Europe have become "vulgar instruments" in the hands of the democracies. As a result, Putin exclaims, "No one feels safe! Because no one can feel that international law is like a stone wall that will protect them."[104]

The western democracies would deny any such intention, but Putin, like the leaders of China, is right to worry. American and European policymakers constantly say they want Russia and China to integrate themselves into the international liberal democratic order, but it is not surprising if Russian and Chinese leaders are wary. Can autocrats enter the liberal international order without succumbing to the forces of liberalism?

Afraid of the answer, the autocracies are understandably pushing back, and with some effect. Rather than accepting the new principles of diminished sovereignty and weakened international protection for autocrats, Russia and China are promoting an international order that places a high value on national sovereignty and can protect autocratic governments from foreign interference.

And they are succeeding. Autocracy is making a comeback. Changes in the ideological complexion of the most influential world powers have always had some effect on the choices made by leaders in smaller nations. Fascism was in vogue in Latin America in the 1930s and 1940s partly because it seemed successful in Italy, Germany, and Spain. Communism spread in the Third World in the 1960s and 1970s not so much because the Soviet Union worked hard to spread it but because government opponents fought their rebellions under the banner of Marxism-Leninism and then enlisted the aid of Moscow. When communism died in Moscow, communist rebellions around the world became few and far between. And if the rising power of the world's democracies in the late years of the Cold War, culminating in their almost total victory after 1989, contributed to the wave of democratization in the 1980s and 1990s, it is logical to expect that the rise of two powerful autocracies should shift the balance back again.

It is a mistake to believe that autocracy has no international appeal. Thanks to decades of remarkable growth, the Chinese today can argue that their model of economic development, which combines an increasingly open economy with a closed political system, can be a successful option for development in many nations. It certainly offers a model for successful autocracy, a blueprint for how to create wealth and stability without having to give way to political liberalization. Russia's model of "sovereign democracy" is attractive among the autocrats of Central Asia. Some Europeans worry that Russia is "emerging as an ideological alternative to the EU that offers a different approach to sovereignty, power and world order."[105] In the 1980s and 1990s, the autocratic model seemed like a losing proposition as dictatorships of both right and left fell before the liberal tide. Today, thanks to the success of China and Russia, it looks like a better bet.

China and Russia may no longer actively export an ideology, but they can and do offer autocrats somewhere to run when the democracies turn hostile. When Iran's relations with Europe plummeted in the 1990s after its clerics issued a fatwa calling for the death of Salman Rushdie, the influential Iranian leader Akbar Hashemi Rafsanjani made a point of noting how much easier it is to maintain good relations with a nation like China.[106] When the dictator of Uzbekistan came under criticism in 2005 from the administration of George W. Bush for violently suppressing an opposition rally, he responded by joining the Shanghai Cooperation Organization and moving closer to Moscow. The Chinese provide unfettered aid to dictatorships in Africa and Asia, undermining the efforts of the "international community" to press for reforms—which in practical terms often means regime change—in countries such as Burma and Zimbabwe. Americans and Europeans may grumble, but autocracies are not in the business of overthrowing other autocrats at the democratic world's insistence. The Chinese, who used deadly force to crack down on student demonstrators not so long ago, will hardly help the West remove a government in Burma for doing the same thing. Nor will they impose conditions on aid to African nations to demand political and institutional reforms they have no intention of carrying out in China.

Chinese officials may chide Burma's rulers; they may urge the Sudanese government to find some solution to the Sudan conflict. Moscow may at times distance itself from Iran. But the rulers in Rangoon, Khartoum, Pyongyang, and Tehran know that their best and, in the last resort, only protectors in a generally hostile world are to be found in Beijing and Moscow. In the great schism between democracy and autocracy, the autocrats share common interests and a common view of international order. As China's Li Peng told Rafsanjani, China and Iran are united by a common desire to build a world order in which "the selection of whatever social system by a country is the affair of the people of that country."[107]

In fact, a global competition is under way. According to Russia's foreign minister, Sergei Lavrov, "For the first time in many years, a real competitive environment has emerged on the market of ideas" between different "value systems and development models." And the good news, from the Russian point of view, is that "the West is losing its monopoly on the globalization process." Today when Russians speak of a multipolar world, they are not only talking about the redistribution of power. It is also the competition of value systems and ideas that will provide "the foundation for a multipolar world order."[108]

This comes as a surprise to a democratic world that believed such competition ended when the Berlin Wall fell. The world's democracies do not regard their own efforts to support democracy and Enlightenment principles abroad as an aspect of a geopolitical competition, because they do not see "competing truths," only "universal values." As a result, they are not always conscious of how they use their wealth and power to push others to accept their values and principles. In their own international institutions and alliances, they demand strict fidelity to liberal democratic principles. Before opening their doors to new members, and before providing the vast benefits that membership offers in terms of wealth and security, they demand that nations who want to enter the EU or NATO open up their economies and political systems. When the Georgian president called a state of emergency at the end of 2007, he damaged Georgia's chances of entering NATO and the EU anytime soon. As a result, Georgia may now live precariously in the nether region between Russian autocracy and European liberalism. Eventually, if the democracies turn their backs on Georgia, it may have no choice but to accommodate Moscow.

This competition is not quite the Cold War redux. It is more like the nineteenth century redux. In the nineteenth century, the absolutist rulers of Russia and Austria shored up fellow autocracies in postrevolutionary France and used force to suppress liberal rebellions in Germany, Poland, Italy, and Spain. Palmerston's Britain used British power to aid liberals on the continent; the United States cheered on liberal revolutions in Hungary and Germany and expressed outrage when Russian troops suppressed liberal forces in Poland. Today Ukraine has already been a battleground between forces supported by the West and forces supported by Russia and could well be a battleground again in the future. Georgia could be another. It is worth contemplating what the world would look like, what Europe would look like, if democratic movements in Ukraine and Georgia failed or were forcefully suppressed and the two nations became autocracies with close ties to Moscow. It is worth considering what the effect would be in East Asia if China used force to quash a democratic system in Taiwan and install a friendlier autocracy in its place.

It may not come to war, but the global competition between democratic and autocratic governments will become a dominant feature of the twenty-first-century world. The great powers are increasingly choosing up sides and identifying themselves with one camp or the other. India, which during the Cold War was proudly neutral or even pro-Soviet, has begun to identify itself as part of the democratic West.[109] Japan in recent years has also gone out of its way to position itself as a democratic great power, sharing common values with other Asian democracies but also with non-Asian democracies. For both

Japan and India the desire to be part of the democratic world is genuine, but it is also part of a geopolitical calculation—a way of cementing solidarity with other great powers that can be helpful in their strategic competition with autocratic China.

There is no perfect symmetry in international affairs. The twin realities of the present era—great power competition and the contest between democracy and autocracy—will not always produce the same alignments. Democratic India in its geopolitical competition with autocratic China supports the Burmese dictatorship in order to deny Beijing a strategic advantage. India's diplomats enjoy playing the other great powers off against each other, sometimes warming to Russia, sometimes to China. Democratic Greece and Cyprus pursue close relations with Russia partly out of cultural solidarity with Eastern Orthodox cousins but more out of economic interest. The United States has long allied itself to Arab dictatorships for strategic and economic reasons, as well as to successive military rulers in Pakistan. Just as during the Cold War, strategic and economic considerations, as well as cultural affinities, may often cut against ideology.

But in today's world, a nation's form of government, not its "civilization" or its geographical location, may be the best predictor of its geopolitical alignment. Asian democracies today line up with European democracies against Asian autocracies. Chinese observers see a "V-shaped belt" of pro-American democratic powers "stretching from Northeast to Central Asia."[110] When the navies of India, the United States, Japan, Australia, and Singapore exercised in the Bay of Bengal last year, Chinese and other observers referred to it as the "axis of democracy."[111] Japan's prime minister spoke of an "Asian arc of freedom and prosperity" stretching from Japan to Indonesia to India.[112] Russian officials profess to be "alarmed" that NATO and the Organization for Security and Cooperation in Europe are "reproducing a bloc policy" not unlike that of the Cold War era. But the Russians themselves refer to the Shanghai Cooperation Organization as an "anti-NATO" alliance and a "Warsaw Pact 2."[113] When the Shanghai Cooperation Organization met last year, it brought together five autocracies—China, Russia, Uzbekistan, Kazakhstan, and Tajikistan—as well as Iran.[114] When the ASEAN nations attempted to address the problem of Burma last year, the organization split down the middle, with democratic nations like the Philippines and Indonesia, backed by Japan, seeking to put pressure on Burma, and the autocracies of Vietnam, Cambodia, and Laos, backed by China, seeking to avoid setting a precedent that could come back to haunt them someday.[115]

The divisions between the United States and its European allies that opened wide after the invasion of Iraq are being overshadowed by these more fundamental geopolitical divisions, and especially by growing tensions between the democratic transatlantic alliance and autocratic Russia. European attitudes toward Russia are hardening. But so are European attitudes toward China. Polls show that in Britain, Germany, France, and Spain, China's image has been plummeting in recent years. Only 34 percent of Germans had a favorable view of Beijing in 2007,[116] which may explain why Chancellor Angela Merkel felt free to incur China's ire last year by meeting with the Dalai Lama.

This does not mean Americans and Europeans will agree on how best to handle relations with Moscow or Beijing. China is well beyond Europe's daily strategic concern, and Europeans are therefore more inclined to accommodate China's rise than are Americans, Indians, or Japanese. When it comes to Russia, Europeans may want to pursue an accommodating *Ostpolitik,* as they did during the Cold War, rather than a more confrontational American-style approach. But the trends in Europe are toward greater democratic solidarity. Leading politicians in Germany talk of broadening their nation's approach to Asia, focusing not only on "economic ties" with China but also on "values" and seeking closer strategic relations with "South Korea, Japan, India and Indonesia [who] can play a role in security and other big global issues."[117]

The autocracies of Egypt and Saudi Arabia remain closely tied to Washington, and at least one recent democratic election, in Palestine, produced an anti-American majority. Because many Arab Muslims view the United States as the latest of the western powers to oppress them, this is not surprising. The question is, how long will the Middle East remain the exception? It is possible that over time Egypt and Saudi Arabia may see virtue in drawing closer to their fellow autocrats in Moscow and Beijing. It is also possible that a more democratic Lebanon, a more democratic Iraq, and a more democratic Morocco may form a new bloc of pro-American democracies in the region, alongside the more moderate, democratizing autocracies of Kuwait, Jordan, and Bahrain.

The global divisions between the club of autocrats and the axis of democracy have broad implications for the international system. Is it possible any longer to speak of an "international community"? The term implies agreement on international norms of behavior, an international morality, even an international conscience. Today the world's major powers lack such a common understanding. On the large strategic questions, such as whether to intervene or impose sanctions or attempt to isolate nations diplomatically, there is no longer an international community to be summoned or led. This was exposed most blatantly in the war over Kosovo, which divided the democratic West from both Russia and China, and from many other non-European autocracies. Today it is apparent on the issues of Darfur, Iran, and Burma.

One would imagine that on such transnational issues as disease, poverty, and climate change the great powers ought to be able to work together despite their diverging interests and worldviews. But even here their differences complicate matters. Disputes between the democracies and China over how and whether to condition aid to poor countries in Africa affect the struggle against poverty. Geopolitical calculations affect international negotiations over the best response to climate change. The Chinese, along with the Indians, believe the advanced industrial nations of the West, having reached their present heights after decades of polluting the air and emitting unconscionable levels of greenhouse gases, now want to deny others the right to grow in the same way. Beijing suspects a western attempt to restrict China's growth and slow its emergence as a competitive great power.

The nuclear nonproliferation regime will continue to suffer as the clashing interests of great powers and differing forms of government overwhelm what might otherwise be their common interests in preventing other nations from obtaining nuclear weapons. Russia and China have run interference for Iran. The United States has run interference for India, in order to enlist New Delhi's help in the strategic competition with China.

The demise of the international community is most clearly on display at the United Nations Security Council, which, after a brief post–Cold War awakening, is slipping back into its long coma. The artful diplomacy of France and the tactical caution of China for a while obscured the fact that on most major issues the Security Council has been sharply divided between the autocracies and the democracies, with the latter systematically pressing for sanctions and other punitive actions against autocracies in Iran, North Korea, Sudan, and Burma, and the former just as systematically resisting and attempting to weaken the effect of such actions. This rut will only deepen in the coming years.

Calls for a new "concert" of nations in which Russia, China, the United States, Europe, and other great powers establish some kind of international condominium are unlikely to be successful. The early-nineteenth-century Concert of Europe operated under the umbrella of a common morality and shared principles of government. It aimed not only at the preservation of a European peace but also, and more important, at the maintenance of a monarchical and aristocratic order against the liberal and radical challenges presented by the French and American revolutions and their echoes in Germany, Italy, and Poland. The concert gradually broke down under the strains of popular nationalism, fueled in part by the rise of revolutionary liberalism. The great power concert that Franklin Roosevelt established at the UN Security Council similarly foundered on ideological conflict.

Today there is little sense of shared morality and common values among the great powers. Instead there is suspicion and growing hostility, and the well-grounded view on the part of the autocracies that the democracies, whatever they say, would welcome their overthrow. Any concert among these states would be built on a shaky foundation likely to collapse at the first serious test.

Can these disagreements be overcome by expanding trade ties and growing economic interdependence in this ever more globalized world? Clearly economic ties can help check tendencies toward great power conflict. Chinese leaders avoid confrontation with the United States today both because they could not count on a victory and because they fear the impact on the Chinese economy and, by extension, the stability of their autocratic rule. American, Australian, and Japanese dependence on the Chinese economy makes these nations cautious, too, and the powerful influence of American big business makes American leaders take a more accommodating view of China. In both China and Russia, economic interests are not just national but also personal. If the business of Russia is business, as Dmitri Trenin argues, its leaders should be reluctant to jeopardize their wealth with risky foreign policies.

Yet history has not been kind to the theory that strong trade ties prevent conflict between nations. The United States and China are no more dependent on each other's economies today than were Great Britain and Germany before World War I. And trade relations are not without their own tensions and conflicts. Those between the United States and China are becoming increasingly contentious, with the U.S. Congress threatening legislation to punish China for perceived inequities in the trade relationship. In both Europe and the United States, concerns about the growing strategic challenge from China are increasingly joined or even outstripped by fears of the growing economic challenge it poses. Fifty-five percent of Germans believe China's economic growth is a "bad thing," up from 38 percent in 2005, a view shared by Americans, Indians, Britons, the French, and even South Koreans. Today 60 percent of South Koreans think China's growing economy is a "bad thing."[118]

The Chinese, meanwhile, may still tolerate pressure to adjust their currency, crack down on piracy, and increase quality standards of their products, as well as all the other hectoring they receive from the United States and Europe. But they are starting to feel that the democratic world is ganging up on them and using these disputes as a way of containing China not only economically but strategically.

Finally, there is the international scramble for energy resources, which is becoming the primary arena for geopolitical competition. The search for reliable sources of oil and gas shapes China's policies toward Iran, Sudan, Burma, and Central Asia. Russia and the democracies led by the United States compete to build oil and gas pipelines that will provide them leverage and influence, or deny it to their competitors.

Commercial ties alone cannot withstand the forces of national and ideological competition that have now so prominently reemerged. Trade relations don't take place in a vacuum. They both influence and are influenced by geopolitical and ideological conflicts. Nations are not calculating machines. They have the attributes of the humans who create and live in them, the intangible and immeasurable human qualities of love, hate, ambition, fear, honor, shame, patriotism, ideology, and belief, the things people fight and die for, today as in millennia past.

THE HOPELESS DREAM
OF RADICAL ISLAM

NOWHERE ARE THESE HUMAN QUALITIES more on display than in the Islamic world, especially in the Middle East. The struggle of radical Islamists against the powerful and often impersonal forces of modernization, capitalism, and globalization that they associate with the Judeo-Christian West is the other great conflict in the international system today. It is also the most dramatic refutation of the convergence paradigm, since it is precisely convergence, including the liberal world's conception of "universal values," that the radical Islamists reject.

As a historical phenomenon, the struggle between

modernization and Islamic radicalism may ultimately have less impact on international affairs than the struggle among the great powers and between the forces of democracy and autocracy. Islamic resistance to westernization is not a new phenomenon, after all, though it has taken on a new and potentially cataclysmic dimension. In the past, when old and less technologically advanced peoples confronted more advanced cultures, their inadequate weapons reflected their backwardness. Today, the more radical proponents of Islamic traditionalism, though they abhor the modern world, are nevertheless not only using the ancient methods of assassination and suicidal attacks, but also have deployed the weapons of the modern world against it. The forces of modernization and globalization have inflamed the radical Islamist rebellion and also armed them for the fight.

It is a lonely and ultimately desperate fight, however, for in the struggle between traditionalism and modernity, tradition cannot win—even though traditional forces armed with modern weapons, technologies, and ideologies can do horrendous damage. All the world's rich and powerful nations have more or less embraced the economic, technological, and even social aspects of modernization and globalization. All have embraced, albeit with varying degrees of complaint and resistance, the free flow of goods, finances, and services, and the intermingling of cultures and lifestyles that characterize the modern world. Increasingly, their people watch the same television shows, listen to the same music, and go to the same movies. Along with this dominant modern culture, they have accepted, even as they may also deplore, the essential characteristics of a modern morality and aesthetics. Modernity means, among other things, the sexual as well as political and economic liberation of women, the weakening of church authority and the strengthening of secularism, the existence of what used to be called the counterculture, and free expression in the arts (if not in politics), which includes the freedom to commit blasphemy and to lampoon symbols of faith, authority, and morality. These are the consequences of liberalism and capitalism unleashed and unchecked by the constraining hand of tradition, a powerful church, or a moralistic and domineering government. Even the Chinese have learned that while it is possible to have capitalism without political liberalization, it is much harder to have capitalism without cultural liberalization.

Today radical Islamists are the last holdout against these powerful forces of modernity. For Sayyid Qutb, one of the intellectual fathers of Al Qaeda, true Islam could be salvaged only by warring against the modern world on all fronts. He wanted to "take apart the entire political and philosophical structure of modernity and return Islam to its unpolluted origins."[119] A very different kind of Muslim leader, Ayatollah Khomeini, clearly identified modernity with the Enlightenment and rejected both. "Yes, we are reactionaries," he told his opponents, "and you are enlightened intellectuals: You intellectuals do not want us to go back 1,400 years."[120]

These most radical Islamists, along with Osama bin Laden, also reject that great product of the Enlightenment and modernity: democracy. Abu Musab al-Zarqawi denounced elections in Iraq on the grounds that "the legislator who must be obeyed in a democracy is man, and not God." Democratic elections were "the very essence of heresy and polytheism and error," for they made "the weak, ignorant man God's partner in His most central divine prerogative—namely, ruling and legislating." As Bernard Lewis has written, the aim of Islamic revolution in Iran and elsewhere has been to "sweep away all the alien and infidel accretions that had been imposed on the Muslim lands and peoples in the era of alien dominance and influence and to restore the true and divinely given Islamic order." One of those "infidel accretions" is democracy. The fundamentalists want to take the Islamic world back to where they were before the Christian West, liberalism, and modernity polluted pure Islam.[121]

That goal is impossible to achieve. The Islamists could not take their societies back 1,400 years even if the rest of the world would let them. And it won't let them. Neither the United States nor any of the other great powers will turn over control of the Middle East to these fundamentalist forces. Partly this is because the region is of such vital strategic importance to the rest of the world. But it is more than that. The vast majority of the people in the Middle East have no desire to go back 1,400 years. They oppose neither modernity nor democracy. Nor is it conceivable in this modern world that a whole country could wall itself off from modernity, even if the majority wanted to do so. Could the great Islamic theocracy that Al Qaeda and others hope to erect ever completely block out the sights and sounds of the rest of the world, and thereby shield their people from the temptations of modernity? The mullahs have not even succeeded in doing that in Iran. The project is fantastic.

The world is thus faced with the prospect of a protracted struggle in which the goals of the extreme Islamists can never be satisfied because neither the United States, nor Europe, nor Russia, nor China, nor the peoples of the Middle East have the ability or the desire to give them what they want. The modern great powers are quite simply not capable of retreating as far as the Islamic extremists require.

Unfortunately, they may also not be capable of uniting effectively against the threat. Although in the struggle between modernization and tradition, the United States, Russia, China, Europe, and the other great powers are roughly on the same side, the things that divide them from one another—the competing national ambitions, the divisions between democrats and autocrats, the trans- atlantic disagreement over the use of military power— undermine their will to cooperate. This is certainly true when it comes to the unavoidable military aspects of a fight against radical Islamic terrorism. Europeans have been and will continue to be less than enthusiastic about what they emphatically do not call "the war on terror." As for Russia and China, it will be tempting for them to enjoy the spectacle of the United States bogged down in a fight with Al Qaeda and other violent Islamist groups in the Middle East and South Asia, just as it is tempting to let American power in that region be checked by a nuclear- armed Iran. The willingness of the autocrats in Moscow and Beijing to protect their fellow autocrats in Pyongyang,

Tehran, and Khartoum increases the chances that the connection between terrorists and nuclear weapons will eventually be made.

Indeed, one of the problems with making the struggle against Islamic terrorism the sole focus of American foreign policy is that it produces illusions about alliance and cooperation with other great powers with whom genuine alliance is becoming impossible. The idea of genuine strategic cooperation between the United States and Russia or the United States and China in the war on terror is mostly a fiction. For Russia, the war on terror is about Chechnya. For China it is about the Uyghurs of Xinjiang province. But when it comes to Iran, Syria, and Hezbollah, Russia and China tend to see not terrorists but useful partners in the great power struggle.

THE VICES AND VIRTUES OF AMERICAN HEGEMONY

WHAT ROLE SHOULD THE UNITED STATES play in such a world? Global public opinion polls suggest a strong international desire for a diminished American role, a move toward greater multipolarity and equality in the international system. In the United States itself, there are calls for humility, for a tempering of ambitions and a greater sense of limits. In the wake of the Iraq War, the world has been preoccupied with the "American problem." And no doubt there is an American problem, due to errors of commission and omission, not only in recent years but throughout America's history. The tendency toward unilateralism, the suspicion of international institutions, the jealous clinging to national sovereignty, the greater proclivity to use force to address international problems, as well as the noble generosity of spirit and perception of enlightened self-interest that lead the United States out into the world to assist others—these enduring qualities of American foreign policy were not invented by the Bush administration and will not vanish when it departs.

But whether American power and expansiveness will continue to be the most pressing problem in the years to come, or whether it is the most pressing problem even today, is increasingly debatable. In a world heading toward a more perfect liberal order, an old-fashioned superpower with a sense of global mission might seem a relic of the past and an obstacle to progress. But in a world poised precariously at the edge of a new time of turmoil, might not even a flawed democratic superpower have an important, even indispensable, role to play?

As it happens, American predominance is unlikely to fade anytime soon, largely because much of the world does not really want it to. Despite the opinion polls, America's relations with both old and new allies have actually strengthened in recent years. Despite predictions that other powers would begin to join together in an effort to balance against the rogue superpower, especially after the Iraq War, the trend has gone in the opposite direction.

China and Russia have been working together to balance against the United States. But there are obstacles to a lasting strategic alliance between the two powers. They have entered into an arms alliance, if not a formal strategic alliance, with Russia selling billions of dollars' worth of advanced military technology and weaponry to the Chinese for use against the United States in any conflict that may arise. They have strengthened the Shanghai Cooperation Organization as an increasingly military as well as political institution. Yet they also remain traditional rivals. Russians continue to fear that the massive and productive Chinese population will quietly overrun Russia's sparsely populated Siberian and far eastern territory. China's manufacturing economy, meanwhile, is more dependent on the American market than is the oil-exporting Russia. Russian leaders sometimes fear that the Chinese love the American market more than they hate American hegemony. But for the time being, the geopolitical interests of the two great powers align more than they diverge. They both have an interest and a desire to reduce the scale of American predominance and to create a more equal distribution of power in the world, which is another way of saying they want more relative power for themselves.

Their problem is that the world's other great powers— the democratic powers of Europe, Japan, and India—are unwilling to go along. On the contrary, they are drawing closer to the United States geopolitically. The most striking change has occurred in India, a former ally of Moscow that today sees good relations with the United States as essential to achieving its broader strategic and economic goals. India's foreign ministry spokesman put it simply: "The U.S. is the dominant superpower, so it is logical that we should seek to develop good relations with it."[122] Japanese leaders came to that conclusion a decade ago. In the mid-1990s, the Japanese-American alliance was in danger of eroding. But since 1997 the strategic relationship between the two countries has grown stronger, partly because of Japan's escalating concerns about China and North Korea, and partly as a means of enhancing Japan's own position in East Asia and the world. Some of the nations of Southeast Asia have also begun hedging against a rising China. And even South Korea, with its complex relationship with the United States and hostile relationship with Japan, has begun to eye China warily. A remarkable 89 percent of South Koreans polled last year said they believed China's growing military power was a "bad thing."[123]

In Europe there is also an unmistakable trend toward closer strategic relations with the United States. A few years ago, Gerhard Schroeder and Jacques Chirac flirted with drawing closer to Russia as a way of counterbalancing American power. But now France, Germany, and the rest of Europe have been moving in the other direction. This is not out of renewed affection for the United States. It is a response to changing international circumstances and to lessons learned from the past. The more pro-American foreign policies of Nicolas Sarkozy and Angela Merkel are not only a matter of their unique personalities but also reflect a reassessment of French, German, and European interests. Close but not uncritical relations with the United States, they believe, give a boost to European power and influence that Europe cannot achieve on its own. The Chirac-Schroeder attempt to make Europe a counterweight to American power failed in part because the European Union's newest members from Central and Eastern Europe fear a resurgent Russia and insist on close strategic ties with Washington.

As Russia and China have learned to their chagrin, the great and continuing divide between American and European views of the role of power and the use of force will not produce a strategic decoupling of Europe and the United States. "If you asked me which of the [two] countries France will have closer relations with—the United States or Russia," Sarkozy has said, " 'the U.S.' would be my answer. . . . The friendship between Europe and the United States is a cornerstone of world stability, period."[124] On balance, traditional allies of the United States in East Asia and in Europe, while their publics may be more anti-American than in the past, are nevertheless pursuing policies that reflect greater concern about the powerful autocratic states in their midst than about the United States.[125] With the split over Iraq fading, Russia's foreign minister today worries about the "consolidation of the transatlantic link at our expense."[126]

Even in the Middle East, where anti-Americanism runs hottest and where images of the American occupation in Iraq and memories of Abu Ghraib continue to burn in the popular memory, the strategic balance has not shifted very much. Jordan, Egypt, Saudi Arabia, and Morocco continue to work closely with the United States, despite somewhat greater pressure emanating from Washington for political reform of these autocracies. So, too, do the nations of the Persian Gulf organized in the Gulf Cooperation Council, who are worried about Iran. Libya has moved from being squarely in the anti-American camp to a more ambiguous posture. Lebanon remains a battleground but is arguably closer to the United States today than it was when more fully under Syria's thumb a few years ago. Iraq has shifted from implacable anti-Americanism under Saddam Hussein to dependence on the United States. A stable, pro-American Iraq would shift the strategic balance in a decidedly pro-American direction. Iraq sits on vast oil reserves and could become a significant power in the region.

This favorable strategic balance could shift suddenly and dramatically. If Iran obtains a nuclear weapon and the means to deliver it, that will transform the strategic equation in the region. In the meantime, however, like Russia and China, Iran itself faces some regional balancing. An alliance of Sunni states worries about the expanding Iranian and Shiite influence in the Middle East. Along with Israel, and backed by the American superpower, this anti-Iranian coalition seems stronger than any anti-American coalition Iran has been able to assemble.[127] Despite efforts to expand its own alliances in the region, Iran has only Syria. Iranian-backed resistance movements like Hezbollah and Hamas continue to gather strength, but they have yet to produce a strategic revolution in the region.

This lack of fundamental realignment in the Middle East contrasts sharply with the major strategic setbacks the United States suffered during the Cold War. In the 1950s and 1960s, the pan-Arab nationalist movement swept across the region and opened the door to unprecedented Soviet involvement, including a quasi-alliance between Moscow and the Egypt of Gamal Abdel Nasser, as well as Syria. In 1979, a key pillar of the American strategic position in the region toppled when the pro-American shah of Iran was overthrown by Ayatollah Khomeini's virulently anti-American revolution. That led to a fundamental shift in the strategic balance in the region from which the United States is still suffering. Nothing similar has yet occurred as a result of the Iraq War.

Meanwhile, the number of overseas American military bases continues to grow in the Middle East and elsewhere. Since September 11, 2001, the United States has built or expanded bases in Afghanistan, Kyrgyzstan, Pakistan, Tajikistan, and Uzbekistan in Central Asia; in Bulgaria, Georgia, Hungary, Poland, and Romania in Europe; as well as in the Philippines, Djibouti, Oman, Qatar, and of course, Iraq. In the 1980s hostility to the American military presence began forcing the United States out of the Philippines and in the 1990s seemed to be undermining support for American bases in Japan. Today, the Philippines is rethinking that decision, and the furor over U.S. bases in Japan has largely subsided. In Germany, American bases are less controversial than American plans to reduce them. This is not what one would expect if there was a widespread fear or hatred of overweening American power. Much of the world not only tolerates but willingly lends its support to American geopolitical primacy, not because people love America, but as protection against more worrying regional powers.[128]

Chinese strategists believe the present international

configuration is likely to endure for some time, and they are probably right. So long as the United States remains at the center of the international economy, the predominant military power, and the leading apostle of the world's most popular political philosophy; so long as the American public continues to support American predominance, as it has consistently for six decades; and so long as potential challengers inspire more fear than sympathy among their neighbors, the structure of the international system should remain as it has been, with one superpower and several great powers.[129]

Is this a good thing? The answer is: Compared to what? Compared to a more perfect international liberal order in which nations are more equal, more liberal, more democratic, more committed to peace, and more obedient to the dictates of international rules and norms, the present American-dominated order may be inferior. The United States unfortunately is not immune to all the normal human and national foibles, including arrogance and selfishness and also, at times, excessive humility and the mistakes that come from trying to be too unselfish. It sometimes acts when it shouldn't, and other times it fails to act when it should. It commits errors of judgment as well as errors of execution, just as other nations do. But because of its size and importance in the international system, its errors can rock the planet in ways that the errors of lesser powers do not. As others have observed many times over the past century, the United States is like a big dog in a small room: When it wags its tail, things get knocked over. When the United States performs ineptly, as in Iraq, the effects ripple across the globe. When it bends international norms, as great powers sometimes do, it can have a much greater effect on the international system than when smaller nations do the same thing.

But even if the United States were superhuman in its wisdom, even if it behaved morally and capably at all times, American power would still inspire jealousy and hostility and, in some quarters, even fear. The American-dominated order blocks the path of other nations who would naturally prefer a distribution of power and influence more favorable to their own interests—China, Russia, and Iran, for instance. But it poses difficulties even for those, like the Europeans, who are relatively comfortable with the overall distribution of power in the world but uncomfortable with a United States they cannot control. This is not a new problem. Even in the early years of the Cold War, now recalled as a time of blissful transatlantic harmony, Europeans feared the power of their American benefactors and worried that, as one statesman put it, "we would be too impotent to correct you when you are wrong and you would be too idealistic to correct yourself."[130]

The flaws in the present system are obvious enough. But what is the realistic alternative? People may hope for a more harmonious world based on a new concert of nations, but the rise of great power competition and the clashing interests and ambitions of nations across Eurasia make such an evolution unlikely. Even under the umbrella of American predominance, regional conflicts involving the large powers may erupt. The question is whether a less dominant America would make such conflicts less likely or more likely. The United States can and does act selfishly and obtusely, disturbing or even harming the interests of other nations. But it is not clear that in a multipolar world Russia, China, India, Japan, or even Europe would be wiser or more virtuous in the exercise of its power. One novel aspect of such a multipolar world would be that most of these powers would possess nuclear weapons. That could make wars between them less likely, or it could make them more catastrophic.

In East Asia, most nations agree that a reliable and predominant America has a stabilizing and pacific effect. Even China, which seeks gradually to supplant the United States as the dominant power in the region, faces the dilemma that an American withdrawal could unleash an ambitious, independent, nationalist Japan.

In Europe, too, the withdrawal of the United States from the scene—even if it remained the world's most powerful nation—could be destabilizing. It could tempt Russia to an even more overbearing and potentially forceful approach to unruly nations on its periphery. If the United States pulled back from Europe, this could in time increase the likelihood of conflict involving Russia and its near neighbors. The European Union, that great geopolitical miracle, owes its founding to American power. Without it, France, the United Kingdom, and others would never have felt secure enough after World War II to reintegrate Germany into Europe. And although most Europeans recoil at the thought, Europe's stability still depends on the guarantee that, in the last resort, the United States could step in to check any dangerous development on the continent.

It is also optimistic to imagine that a diminished American position in the Middle East would lead to greater stability there. The competition for influence among powers both inside and outside the region has raged for at least two centuries. The rise of Islamic fundamentalism only adds a new and more threatening dimension. Neither a sudden end to the conflict between Israel and the Palestinians nor an immediate American withdrawal from Iraq would bring an end to Middle East tensions and competition. To the extent the United States withdraws or reduces its presence, other powers, both inside and outside the region, will fill the vacuum. One can expect deeper involvement in the Middle East by both China and Russia regardless of what the United States does, if only to secure their growing interests and further their growing ambitions. And one could also expect the more powerful states of the region, particularly Iran, to fulfill their old ambition of becoming the region's hegemon.

In most of the vital regions of the world, in East Asia, Europe, and the Middle East, the United States is still the keystone in the arch. Remove it, and the arch collapses.

This is also true in a broader sense. For the past six decades, American power has provided a number of international public goods—services that benefit not only the United States but many other nations, as well. To take one example, the U.S. Navy preserves the safety and freedom of international waterways for all nations, and it does so even when the United States itself is at war. It doesn't have to be this way. Throughout most of history, control of sea lanes and trade routes was constantly contested by the great powers. When they went to war with one another, the entire international commercial system was affected, and neutral nations suffered as much as combatant nations. If allowed to do so, China and India would contest for control of the Indian Ocean, Japan and China might contest for control of the waters between them, and in the event of war the crucial trade routes would be closed not only to these nations but to the entire world. In the absence of American naval predominance, regional conflicts in the Middle East and Persian Gulf could lead to the closure of the Straits of Hormuz and the Suez Canal. If this hasn't happened in recent decades, it is not because the nations of the world have learned, evolved, and adopted new norms of international behavior. It is because the American navy dominates the oceans.

International order does not rest on ideas and institutions alone. It is shaped by configurations of power. The international order of the 1990s reflected the distribution of power in the world after World War II and the Cold War. The order of today reflects the rising influence of the great powers, including the great power autocracies. A different configuration of power, a multipolar world in which the poles were Russia, China, the United States, India, and Europe, would produce its own kind of order, with different rules and norms reflecting the interests of the powerful states that had a hand in shaping it. Would that international order be an improvement? Perhaps for Beijing, Moscow, and Tehran it would. But it is doubtful that it would serve the interests of Enlightenment democrats in the United States and Europe as well as the present system does.

TOWARD A CONCERT OF DEMOCRACIES

THE WORLD'S DEMOCRACIES NEED to begin thinking about how they can protect their interests and defend their principles in a world in which these are once again powerfully challenged. This will include establishing new means of gauging and granting international legitimacy to actions. The United Nations Security Council cannot serve this purpose because it has become hopelessly paralyzed by the split between its autocratic and democratic members. Yet the democratic world will still need mechanisms to reconcile differences and reach consensus. One possibility might be to establish a global concert or league of democracies, perhaps informally at first, but with the aim of holding regular meetings and consultations among democratic nations on the issues of the day. Such an institution could bring together Asian and Pacific nations such as Japan, Australia, and India with the EU and NATO nations of Europe and North America, along with other democracies, such as Brazil—democracies that have until now had comparatively little to do with each other outside the realms of trade and finance. The institution would complement, not replace, the United Nations, NATO, the G8, and other global organizations. But it would signal a commitment to the democratic idea, and it could become a means of pooling the resources of democratic nations to address a number of issues that cannot be addressed at the United Nations. If successful, it could help bestow legitimacy on actions that democratic nations deem necessary but autocratic nations refuse to countenance—as NATO conferred legitimacy on the intervention in Kosovo.

In a world increasingly divided along democratic and autocratic lines, the world's democrats will have to stick together. This does not require a blind crusade on behalf of democracy everywhere at all times, or a violent confrontation with the autocratic powers. Democracies need not stop trading with autocracies or engaging in negotiations with them over matters of both common interest and divergent interest. But the foreign policies of the United States and the democracies need to be attuned to the political distinctions in today's world and recognize the role the struggle between democracy and autocracy plays in the most important strategic questions. True realism about international affairs means understanding that a nation's foreign policy is heavily shaped by the nature of its government. The world's democracies need to show solidarity for one another, and they need to support those trying to pry open a democratic space where it has been closing.

Support for democracy has strategic relevance in part because it plays to the liberal world's strengths and exposes the weaknesses of the autocratic powers. It is easy to look at China and Russia today and believe they are impervious to outside influence. But one should not overlook their fragility and vulnerability. These autocratic regimes may be stronger than they were in the past in terms of wealth and global influence, but they still live in a predominantly democratic era. That means they face an unavoidable problem of legitimacy. They are not like the monarchs of eighteenth- and nineteenth-century Europe, who enjoyed a historical legitimacy because the world had known little else but autocracy for centuries. Today's autocracies struggle to create a new kind of legitimacy, and it is no easy task. Chinese leaders race forward with their economy in fear that any slowing will be their undoing. They fitfully stamp out even the tiniest hints of political opposition because they live in fear of repeating the Soviet collapse and their own near-death experience in 1989. They fear foreign support for any internal political opposition more than they fear foreign invasion. In Russia, Putin strains to obliterate his opponents, even though they appear weak, because he fears that any sign of life in the opposition could bring his regime down.

The world's democracies have a strategic interest in keeping the hopes for democracy alive in Russia and China. The optimists in the early post–Cold War years were not wrong to believe that a democratizing Russia and China would be better international partners. A democratic China is much less likely to find itself in a conflict with the United States, partly because Americans will be more tolerant of a rising great power democracy than of a rising great power autocracy.

The mistake of the 1990s was the hope that democracy was inevitable. Today, excessive optimism has been replaced in many quarters by excessive pessimism. Many Europeans insist that outside influences will have no effect on Russia. Yet, looking back on the Cold War, many of these same Europeans believe that the Helsinki Accords of the 1970s had a subtle but eventually profound impact on the evolution of the Soviet Union and eastern bloc. Is Putin's Russia more impervious to such methods than Leonid Brezhnev's Soviet Union? Putin himself does not think so. Nor do China's rulers, or they wouldn't spend billions policing Internet chat rooms and waging a campaign of repression against the Falun Gong.

Should the United States and others promote democracy in the Middle East, too? One way to answer that question is to turn it around: Should the United States support autocracy in the Middle East? That is the only other choice, after all. There is no neutral stance on such matters. The world's democracies are either supporting autocracy, through aid, recognition, amicable diplomatic relations, and regular economic intercourse, or they are using their manifold influence in varying degrees to push for democratic reform. Policymakers and analysts may argue over the proper pace of reform or the precise amount of pressure to apply, but few Europeans and even fewer Americans would say that the democracies should simply support Middle Eastern autocrats and not push for change at all.

The main questions, then, are really a matter of tactics and timing. But no matter whether one prefers fast or slow, hard or soft, there will always be the danger that pressure of any kind will produce a victory for radical Islamists. Is it worth the risk? A similar question arose constantly during the Cold War, when American liberals called on the United States to stop supporting Third

World dictators, and American conservatives and neocon-servatives warned that the dictators would be replaced by pro-Soviet communists. Sometimes this proved true. But more often such efforts produced moderate democratic governments that were pro-American. The lesson of the Reagan years, when pro-American and reasonably demo-cratic governments replaced right-wing dictatorships in El Salvador, Guatemala, the Philippines, Taiwan, South Korea, and elsewhere, was that the risk was, on balance, worth taking.

It may be worth taking again in the Middle East, and not only as a strategy of democracy promotion but as part of a larger effort to address Islamic radicalism by acceler-ating and intensifying its confrontation with the modern globalized world. Of the many bad options in dealing with this immensely dangerous problem, the best may be to hasten the process—more modernization, more global-ization, faster. This would require greater efforts to sup-port and expand capitalism and the free market in Arab countries, as many have already recommended, as well as efforts to increase public access to the world through tele-vision and the Internet. Nor should it be thought a setback if these modern communication tools are also used to organize radical extremism. That is unavoidable so long as the radical Islamist backlash persists—and it will for some time to come.

Finally, the democratic world should continue to promote political liberalization; support human rights, including the empowerment of women; and use its influ-ence to support a free press and repeated elections that will, if nothing else, continually shift power from the few

to the many. This, too, will produce setbacks. It will provide a channel for popular resentments to express themselves, and for some radical Islamists to take power
through the ballot box. But perhaps this phase is as
unavoidable as the present conflict, and the sooner it is
begun, the sooner a new phase can take its place.[131]

CONCLUSION

THE GREAT FALLACY OF OUR ERA has been the belief
that a liberal international order rests on the triumph of
ideas and on the natural unfolding of human progress. It
is an immensely attractive notion, deeply rooted in the
Enlightenment worldview of which all of us in the liberal
world are the product. Our political scientists posit theories of modernization, with sequential stages of political
and economic development that lead upward toward liberalism. Our political philosophers imagine a grand historical dialectic, in which the battle of worldviews over the
centuries produces, in the end, the correct liberal democratic answer. Naturally, many are inclined to believe that
the Cold War ended the way it did simply because the better worldview triumphed, as it had to, and that the international order that exists today is but the next stage
forward in humanity's march from strife and aggression
toward a peaceful and prosperous coexistence.

Such illusions are just true enough to be dangerous.
Of course there is strength in the liberal democratic idea
and in the free market. In the long run, and all things
being equal, they should prevail over alternative world-

views, both because of their ability to deliver the material goods and, more important, because of their appeal to a most powerful aspect of human nature, the desire for personal autonomy, recognition, and freedom of thought and conscience.

It is logical, too, that a world of liberal democratic states would gradually produce an international order that reflected those liberal and democratic qualities. This has been the Enlightenment dream since the eighteenth century, when Kant imagined a "Perpetual Peace" consisting of liberal republics and built upon the natural desire of all peoples for peace and material comfort. Although some may scoff, it has been a remarkably compelling vision. Its spirit animated the international arbitration movements at the end of the nineteenth century and the worldwide enthusiasm for the League of Nations in the early twentieth century and the United Nations after World War II. It has also been a remarkably durable vision, withstanding the horrors of two world wars, one more disastrous than the other, and then a long Cold War that for a third time dashed expectations of progress toward the ideal.

It is a testament to the vitality of this Enlightenment vision that hopes for a brand-new era in human history again took hold with such force after the fall of Soviet communism. But a little more skepticism was in order. After all, had mankind really progressed so far? The most destructive century in all the millennia of human history was only just concluding; it was not buried back in some deep, dark, ancient past. Our modern, supposedly enlightened, era produced the greatest of horrors—the massive aggressions, the "total wars," the famines, the genocides, the nuclear warfare—and the perpetrators of these horrors were the world's most advanced and enlightened nations. Recognition of this terrible reality—that modernity had produced not greater good but only worse forms of evil—was a staple of philosophical discussion in the twentieth century. What reason was there to believe that after 1989 humankind was suddenly on the cusp of a brand-new order?

The focus on the dazzling pageant of progress at the end of the Cold War ignored the wires and the beams and the scaffolding that had made such progress possible. It failed to recognize that progress was not inevitable but was contingent on events—battles won or lost, social movements successful or crushed, economic practices implemented or discarded. The spread of democracy was not merely the unfolding of certain ineluctable processes of economic and political development. We don't really know whether such an evolutionary process, with predictable stages and known causes and effects, even exists.[132]

What we do know is that the global shift toward democracy coincided with the historical shift in the balance of power toward those nations and peoples who favored the liberal democratic idea, a shift that began with the triumph of the democratic powers over fascism in World War II and was followed by a second triumph of the democracies over communism in the Cold War. The liberal international order that emerged after these two victories reflected the new overwhelming global balance in favor of liberal forces. But those victories were not inevitable, and they need not be lasting. Today, the reemergence of the great autocratic powers, along with the reactionary forces of Islamic radicalism, has weakened that order and threatens to weaken it further in the years and decades to come.

After World War II, another moment in history when hopes for a new kind of international order were rampant, Hans Morgenthau warned against imagining that at some point "the final curtain would fall and the game of power politics would no longer be played."[133] The struggle continued then, and it continues today. Six decades ago American leaders believed the United States had the ability and responsibility to use its power to prevent a slide back to the circumstances that produced two world wars and innumerable national calamities. Reinhold Niebuhr, who always warned against Americans' ambitions and excessive faith in their own power, also believed, with a faith of his own, that "the world problem cannot be solved if America does not accept its full share of responsibility in solving it."[134] Today the United States shares that responsibility with the rest of the democratic world, which is infinitely stronger than it was when World War II ended. The future international order will be shaped by those who have the power and the collective will to shape it. The question is whether the world's democracies will again rise to that challenge.

NOTES

1. This was the title chosen by former President George H. W. Bush and his national security advisor, Brent Scowcroft, for their account of American foreign policy at the end of the Cold War. George Bush and Brent Scowcroft, *A World Transformed* (New York, 1998).

2. Francis Fukuyama, *The End of History and the Last Man* (New York, 1992), p. 211.

3. Quoted in Thomas L. Pangle and Peter J. Ahrensdorf, *Justice Among Nations: On the Moral Basis of Power and Peace* (Lawrence, Kans., 1999), p. 159.

4. "Toward a New World Order," address to a joint session of Congress by President George H. W. Bush, September 11, 1990.

5. Fukuyama, *The End of History and the Last Man,* p. 263.

6. Dmitri V. Trenin, *Getting Russia Right* (Washington, D.C., 2007), p. 70.

7. "All of this could happen because the new democratic forces in the Soviet Union and Eastern Europe understood better than Western realists that democracies posed little threat to one another." Fukuyama, *The End of History and the Last Man,* p. 264.

8. Martin Walker, "The Clinton Doctrine," *The New Yorker,* October 7, 1996.

9. Quoted in Pangle and Ahrensdorf, *Justice Among Nations,* pp. 159–60.

10. Fukuyama, *The End of History and the Last Man,* p. 263.

11. Michael Mandelbaum, *The Ideas That Conquered the World: Peace, Democracy, and Free Markets in the Twenty-first Century* (New York, 2002), p. 374.

12. G. John Ikenberry, "Liberal International Theory in the Wake of 9/11 and American Unipolarity," paper prepared for seminar, "IR Theory, Unipolarity and September 11th—Five Years On," NUPI (Norwegian Institute of International Affairs), Oslo, Norway, February 3–4, 2006.

13. Dean Acheson quoted in Robert L. Beisner, *Dean Acheson: A Life in the Cold War* (Oxford, 2006), p. 372; Second Inaugural Address, William J. Clinton, January 20, 1997.

14. Strobe Talbott, "Hegemon and Proud of It: No Apologies for Being the Only Superpower—and Acting Like It," *Slate,* June 27, 1998 (online).

15. Robert Cooper, "The New Liberal Imperialism," *The Observer,* April 7, 2002.

16. Rosalie Chen, "China Perceives America: Perspectives of International Relations Experts," *Journal of Contemporary China* 12, no. 35 (May 2003), p. 287.

17. World Bank Country Brief, 2007.

18. According to a report by the European Council on Foreign Relations, "Russia has strengthened its political relationships through recruiting big business to act as lobbyists for the Russian cause inside key EU countries. Its state-controlled companies have built partnerships with companies such as EON and BASF in Germany, ENI in Italy, GDF and to a lesser extent Total in France, and Gasunie in the Netherlands. Even in the context of the deteriorating relations with the UK, Russia decided to buy out rather than expropriate Shell and BP in Sakhalin II and Kovykta. Gazprom forced Shell and BP to sell controlling stakes in the projects for less than their market price but retained these companies as minority partners. A Russian expert told us that this sweetening of the pill for BP and Shell was part of a deliberate attempt to build up a pro-Russian lobby. It worked: within weeks of the deal, BP's chief executive Tony Hayward gave interviews to the international media defending the Russian position." See Mark Leonard and Nicu Popescu, "A Power Audit of EU-Russia Relations," report by the European Council on Foreign Relations, November 2007, p. 15.

19. Speech by European Commissioner on Trade Peter Mandelson, "The EU and Russia: Our Joint Political Challenge," Bologna, Italy, April 20, 2007.

20. Trenin, *Getting Russia Right,* p. 93.

21. See Sarah E. Mendelson and Theodore P. Garber, "Failing the Stalin Test," *Foreign Affairs* 85, no. 1 (January/February 2006).

22. Dmitri V. Trenin, "Russia Leaves the West," *Foreign Affairs* 85, no. 4 (July/August 2006), pp. 88–98.

23. Leonard and Popescu, "A Power Audit of EU-Russia Relations," p. 17.

24. Ivan Krastev, "Russia vs. Europe: The Sovereignty Wars," published on the Web site OpenDemocracy, September 5, 2007, http://www.opendemocracy.net/article/globalisation/institutions_government/russia_europe.

25. Speech by President Nicolas Sarkozy to the Fifteenth Ambassadors' Conference, Paris, August 27, 2007.

26. Its "internal rules, values, and its entire governing philosophy" make it "unimaginable for the EU to use oil embargoes, wine embargoes or transport and trade blockades in the way Russia has against Georgia and Moldova." Leonard and Popescu, "A Power Audit of EU-Russia Relations," p. 27.

27. John Vinocur, "Scandinavia's Concern? 'Russia, Russia, Russia,' " *International Herald Tribune,* October 2, 2007, p. 2.

28. In France and Germany, for instance, roughly two-thirds of those polled in 2007 had an "unfavorable" view of Russia. See the report of the Pew Global Attitudes Project, "Global Unease with Major World Powers," released on June 27, 2007, p. 73.

29. Quoted in Vinocur, "Scandinavia's Concern? 'Russia, Russia, Russia,' " p. 2.

30. See Peter Hays Gries, *China's New Nationalism: Pride, Politics, and Diplomacy* (Berkeley, 2005), p. 105: "The dream of a 'prosperous country and a strong army' *(fuguo qiangbing)* still inspires Chinese over a century after it was first promoted by late-Qing-dynasty reformers."

31. Zheng Bijian, "China's 'Peaceful Rise' to Great Power Status," *Foreign Affairs* 84, no. 5 (September/October 2005), p. 22.

32. Chen Zhimin, "Nationalism, Internationalism and Chinese Foreign Policy," *Journal of Contemporary China* 14, no. 42 (February 2005), pp. 36–37.

33. The idea that China should be preeminent in East Asia "remains relatively strong among both elites and ordinary Chinese citizens." Michael D. Swaine and Ashley J. Tellis, *Interpreting China's Grand Strategy, Past, Present, and Future* (Santa Monica, Calif., 2000), p. 15.

34. Charis Dunn-Chan, "China's Imperial Nostalgia Under Attack," BBC News Online, May 11, 2001.

35. Quoted in U.S. Department of Defense annual report to Congress, "Military Power of the People's Republic of China 2007" (Washington, D.C., 2007), p. 7.

36. *China's National Defense in 2006*, Information Office of the State Council of the People's Republic of China, Beijing, December 2006.

37. David Shambaugh, *Modernizing China's Military: Progress, Problems, Prospects* (Berkeley, Calif., 2004), pp. 284–85. As scholars Andrew Nathan and Robert Ross put it, "China is stronger today and its borders are more secure than at any other time in the last 150 years." Andrew J. Nathan and Robert S. Ross, *The Great Wall and the Empty Fortress: China's Search for Security* (New York, 1998), p. 226. Estimates of Chinese military spending are imprecise because the Chinese official budget does not include many expenditures that would be included in most nations' official budgets. Anthony H. Cordesman and Martin Kleiber summarize the various estimates of actual Chinese defense spending in *Chinese Military Modernization and Force Development: Main Report*, Center for Strategic and International Studies working draft, September 7, 2006, p. 20. They make reference to the following assessments: Department of Defense, *Annual Report to Congress: Military Power of the People's Republic of China* (Washington, D.C., 2006), p. 21; Thomas J. Christensen, "China," in Robert J. Ellings and Aaron L. Friedberg, eds., *Strategic Asia: Power and Purpose, 2001–2002* (Seattle, 2001) p. 45; David Shambaugh, "China's Military: Real or Paper Tiger?" *Washington Quarterly* 19, no. 2 (1996), p. 23.

38. Shambaugh, *Modernizing China's Military*, p. 67.

39. Cordesman and Kleiber, *Chinese Military Modernization*, p. 76.

40. The Chinese people are now taught to think "of sea as territory," something they were not taught in the past, and to understand that their " 'sovereignty' includes three million square kilometers of ocean and seas." Shambaugh, *Modernizing China's Military*, p. 67.

41. As Avery Goldstein has commented, the Chinese see themselves less and less as a "suitor" seeking to win foreign favor on foreign terms and more as a "major player" able to negotiate terms of engagement on an equal footing. See Avery Goldstein, "Great Expectations: Interpreting China's Arrival," *International Security* 22, no. 3 (Winter 1997/98), pp. 25–26.

42. Gries, *China's New Nationalism,* p. 51.

43. David Shambaugh, *Beautiful Imperialist: China Perceives America, 1972–1990* (Princeton, N.J., 1991), pp. 252–53.

44. Gries, *China's New Nationalism,* pp. 142–43.

45. Andrew J. Nathan and Bruce Gilley, *China's New Rulers: The Secret Files* (New York, 2002), p. 208.

46. Chen, "China Perceives America," p. 287.

47. Nathan and Gilley, *China's New Rulers,* 217.

48. Quoted in James Mann, *About Face: A History of America's Curious Relationship with China, from Nixon to Clinton* (New York, 2000), pp. 337–38.

49. Chen, "China Perceives America," p. 290.

50. Thomas Berger, "Japan's International Relations: The Political and Security Dimensions," in Samuel S. Kim, ed., *The International Relations of Northeast Asia* (Lanham, Md., 2004), p. 135.

51. Ibid., p. 137.

52. Patrick L. Smith, "Uncertain Legacy: Japanese Nationalism After Koizumi," *International Herald Tribune,* September, 12, 2006.

53. Gries, *China's New Nationalism,* pp. 70, 39.

54. The "Chinese viewed the Japanese as the paradigmatic 'devils' *(guizi)* during World War II, and they continue to view them that way today" (Ibid., p. 10). Distrust of Japan "runs deep" in the Chinese military and "transcends generations" (Shambaugh, *Modernizing China's Military,* p. 301).

55. Mitsuru Kitano, "The Myth of Rising Japanese Nationalism," *International Herald Tribune,* January 12, 2006.

56. Kokubun Ryosei, "Beyond Normalization: Thirty Years of Sino-Japanese Diplomacy," *Gaiko Forum* 2, no. 4 (2003), pp. 31–39, cited in Gries, *China's New Nationalism,* p. 92.

57. Kitano, "The Myth of Rising Japanese Nationalism."

58. C. Raja Mohan, "India's New Foreign Policy Strategy," paper presented at a seminar hosted by the China Reform Forum and the Carnegie Endowment for International Peace, Beijing, May 26, 2006.

59. Ibid.

60. Sunil Khilnani, "The Mirror Asking," *Outlook* (New Delhi), August 21, 2006.

61. C. Raja Mohan, "India and the Balance of Power," *Foreign Affairs* 85, no. 4 (September/October 2005), pp. 17–18.

62. Mohan, "India's New Foreign Policy Strategy."

63. Prime Minister Atal Bihari Vajpayee, letter to President Bill Clinton, reprinted in *Hindu,* May 14, 1998.

64. "China Is Threat Number One," *Times of India,* May 4, 1998.

65. "China's Anti-Satellite Test Worries India," *Times of India,* February 5, 2007.

66. Yong Deng, "Reputation and the Security Dilemma: China Reacts to the China Threat Theory," in Alistair Iain Johnston and Robert Ross, eds., *New Directions in the Study of China Foreign Policy* (Stanford, Calif., 2006), pp. 196–97.

67. See John W. Garver, *Foreign Relations of the People's Republic of China* (Englewood Cliffs, N.J., 1993), pp. 318–19; Mohan, "India and the Balance of Power," p. 30.

68. Mohan, "India and the Balance of Power," p. 30.

69. Joint statement by Prime Minister Shiuzo Abe and Prime Minister Manmohan Singh, New Delhi, August 22, 2007.

70. Ray Takeyh, "Iran: Assessing Geopolitical Dynamics and U.S. Policy Options," testimony before the House Committee on Armed Services, June 8, 2006; Ray Takeyh, "The Iran Puzzle," *The American Prospect,* May 22, 2007.

71. Quoted in Takeyh, "Iran: Assessing Geopolitical Dynamics and U.S. Policy Options."

72. From 1989 to 2001, the United States intervened with significant military force in Panama (1989), Somalia (1992), Haiti (1994), Bosnia (1995–96), Kosovo (1999), and Iraq (1991, 1998).

73. See Melvyn P. Leffler, *A Preponderance of Power: National Security, the Truman Administration, and the Cold War* (Stanford, Calif., 1992).

74. Every American administration in the last half century has attempted to engineer changes of regime throughout the world, from Dwight Eisenhower's CIA-inspired coups in Iran and Guatemala and his planned overthrow of Fidel Castro, which John F. Kennedy attempted to carry out, to Kennedy's own conniving against Ngo Dinh Diem in Vietnam and Rafael Trujillo in the Dominican Republic, to Richard Nixon's meddling in Chile, to Jimmy Carter's call for the ouster of Anastasio Somoza in Nicaragua, to Ronald Reagan's support of anti-communist guerrilla forces in Nicaragua, Angola, Afghanistan, and Cambodia, to George H. W. Bush's invasion of Panama, to Bill Clinton's actions in Somalia, Haiti, and Bosnia.

75. To pick just a few recent examples, the Reagan administration

sought no international authorization for its covert wars in Nicaragua, Cambodia, Afghanistan, and Angola, and it sought neither United Nations nor OAS support for the invasion of Grenada. The administration of the first President Bush invaded Panama without UN authorization and would have gone to war with Iraq without authorization if Russia had vetoed it. The Clinton administration intervened in Haiti without UN authorization, bombed Iraq over the objection of United Nations Security Council permanent members, and went to war in Kosovo without UN authorization.

76. Speech by French foreign minister Hubert M. Védrine at a conference of the French International Relations Institute, Paris, November 3, 1999.

77. Secretary of State Madeleine K. Albright interview on NBC-TV, *Today,* with Matt Lauer, Columbus, Ohio, February 19, 1998, transcript released by Office of the Spokesman, Department of State.

78. See Richard N. Haass, *The Reluctant Sheriff: The United States After the Cold War* (Washington, D.C., 1998).

79. Reinhold Niebuhr, *The Irony of American History* (New York, 1962), pp. 5, 23.

80. Anti-communism was their "ruling passion in foreign affairs," as Norman Podhoretz put in his 1996 essay "Neo-Conservatism: A Eulogy," *Commentary,* March 1996.

81. Jeane J. Kirkpatrick, "A Normal Country in a Normal Time," *The National Interest,* Fall 1990, pp. 40–44.

82. Trenin, *Getting Russia Right,* 9–10.

83. Krastev, "Russia vs. Europe: The Sovereignty Wars."

84. Trenin, *Getting Russia Right,* pp. 9–10.

85. Leonard and Popescu, "A Power Audit of EU-Russia Relations," p. 13.

86. Krastev, "Russia vs. Europe: The Sovereignty Wars."

87. As Ivan Krastev has put it, "Kremlin-friendly oligarchs will own English soccer clubs and the Russian middle class will freely travel all over Europe but international companies will not be allowed to exploit Russian natural resources and the Kremlin's domestic critics will be expelled from European capitals." Ivan Krastev, "Russia as the 'Other Europe,' " in *Russia in Global Affairs,* no. 4 (October/December 2007).

88. Nathan and Gilley, *China's New Rulers,* p. 236.

89. As two scholars of the subject note, "Economic growth, rather than being a force for democratic change in tyrannical states, can

sometimes be used to strengthen oppressive regimes." Bruce Bueno de Mesquita and George W. Downs, "Development and Democracy," *Foreign Affairs* 84, no. 5 (September/October 2005), pp. 78, 85.

90. Minxin Pei, *China's Trapped Transition: The Limits of Developmental Autocracy* (Cambridge, Mass., 2006).

91. Speech by President Vladimir Putin at the 43rd Munich Conference on Security Policy, February 10, 2007.

92. As the president of Estonia notes, today's Russia has "bad relations with all democratic countries on its borders" and "good relations only with those countries that are undemocratic." Speech by President Toomas Hendrik Ilves at Tbilisi University, May 8, 2007.

93. Yong Deng and Fei-Ling Wang, eds., *China Rising: Power and Motivation in Chinese Foreign Policy* (Lanham, Md., 2004), p. 10.

94. Katrin Bennhold, "New Geopolitics Personified," *International Herald Tribune,* January 24, 2008, p. 10.

95. Speech by President Vladimir Putin at the 43rd Munich Conference on Security Policy.

96. Fei-Ling Wang, "Beijing's Incentive Structure: The Pursuit of Preservation, Prosperity, and Power," in Deng and Wang, *China Rising,* p. 22.

97. Trenin, *Getting Russia Right,* p. 3.

98. Anna Smolchenko, "Putin Lashes Out at West and Domestic Critics at Election Rally," *International Herald Tribune,* November 21, 2007.

99. Cooper, "The New Liberal Imperialism."

100. Shambaugh, *Modernizing China's Military,* p. 298.

101. Speech by President Vladimir Putin at the 43rd Munich Conference on Security Policy.

102. Robert Cooper, *The Breaking of Nations: Order and Chaos in the Twenty-first Century* (London, 2003), pp. 60–61; Henry Kissinger, "The End of NATO as We Know It?" *Washington Post,* August 15, 1999, p. B7.

103. Shambaugh, *Beautiful Imperialist,* p. 274.

104. Speech by President Vladimir Putin at the 43rd Munich Conference on Security Policy.

105. Leonard and Popescu, "A Power Audit of EU-Russia Relations," p. 8.

106. John W. Garver, *China and Iran: Ancient Partners in a Post-Imperial World* (Seattle, 2007), p. 101.

107. Quoted ibid., p. 103.

108. Russian foreign minister Sergei Lavrov, "The Present and the Future of Global Politics," *Russia in Global Affairs,* no. 2 (April/June 2007).

109. See Mohan, "India and the Balance of Power."

110. Liu Xuecheng, "Blueprint for 'Asian NATO,' " *People's Daily,* June 3, 2004.

111. Ignoring the fact that Singapore is not a democracy. Hisane Misake, " 'Axis of Democracy' Flexes Its Military Muscle," *Asia Times,* March 31, 2007 (online).

112. Speech by Prime Minister Shinzo Abe to the Parliament of the Indian Republic, New Delhi, August 22, 2007.

113. Adrian Blomfield, "Putin Praises Strength of 'Warsaw Pact 2,' " *Daily Telegraph,* August 20, 2007.

114. The SCO also includes Kyrgyzstan, which is not an autocracy.

115. Wayne Arnold, "Southeast Asian Pact Exposes Rifts," *New York Times,* November 21, 2007.

116. See the report of the Pew Global Attitudes Project, "Global Unease with Major World Powers," released on June 27, 2007, p. 40.

117. Judy Dempsey, "Germany Looks to Asia, at China's Expense," *International Herald Tribune,* November 20, 2007.

118. See the report of the Pew Global Attitudes Project, "Global Unease with Major World Powers," released on June 27, 2007, pp. 42–43.

119. Lawrence Wright, *The Looming Tower: Al-Qaeda and the Road to 9/11* (New York, 2006), p. 24.

120. Ibid., p. 47.

121. F. Gregory Gause III, "Can Democracy Stop Terrorism?" *Foreign Affairs* 84, no. 5 (September/October 2005), p. 69; Bernard Lewis, *The Middle East* (London, 2000), p. 377.

122. Martine Bulard, "India's Boundless Ambitions," *Le Monde Diplomatique,* January 2007 (online).

123. See the report of the Pew Global Attitudes Project, "Global Unease with Major World Powers," p. 41.

124. Nicolas Sarkozy interview with Europe-1 Radio, May 4, 2007, quoted in RIA Novosti, Moscow, May 7; Sarkozy interview also published in *The National Interest,* July 1, 2007.

125. This is what William Wohlforth predicted almost a decade ago. See William C. Wohlforth, "The Stability of a Unipolar World," *International Security* 24, no. 1 (Summer 1999).

126. Lavrov, "The Present and the Future of Global Politics."

127. Gary G. Sick, interview by Bernard Gwertzman, *Foreign Affairs*, January 23, 2007 (online).

128. For the most thorough discussion of worldwide trends that run counter to the prediction of balancing, see Keir A. Lieber and Gerard Alexander, "Waiting for Balancing: Why the World Is Not Pushing Back," *International Security* 30, no. 1 (Summer 2005).

129. In a 1999 essay, Samuel P. Huntington referred to a "uni-multipolar system with one superpower and several major powers." He expected this to be a short-lived transition to genuine multipolarity. Samuel P. Huntington, "The Lonely Superpower," *Foreign Affairs* 78, no. 2 (March/April 1999).

130. Niebuhr, *The Irony of American History*, p. 133.

131. For the best and most original elaboration of this argument, see Reuel Marc Gerecht, *The Islamic Paradox* (Washington, D.C., 2004).

132. For a cautionary note regarding the various theories concerning the stages of democratic development, see Thomas Carothers, "The 'Sequencing' Fallacy," *Journal of Democracy* 18, no. 1 (January 2007).

133. Hans J. Morgenthau, *Politics Among Nations: The Struggle for Power and Peace* (New York, 1948), p. 20.

134. Reinhold Niebuhr, "American Power and World Responsibility," *Christianity and Crisis*, April 5, 1943, in D. B. Robertson, ed., *Love and Justice: Selections from the Shorter Writings of Reinhold Niebuhr* (Cleveland, 1967), p. 200.

A NOTE ABOUT THE AUTHOR

ROBERT KAGAN is senior associate at the Carnegie
Endowment for International Peace, Transatlantic Fellow
at the German Marshall Fund, a columnist for *The Wash-
ington Post,* and a contributing editor at both *The New
Republic* and *The Weekly Standard.* He is also the author
of *Dangerous Nation: America's Place in the World from Its
Earliest Days to the Dawn of the Twentieth Century; Of
Paradise and Power: America and Europe in the New World
Order; A Twilight Struggle: American Power and Nica-
ragua, 1977-1990;* and editor, with William Kristol, of
*Present Dangers: Crisis and Opportunity in American
Foreign and Defense Policy.* Kagan served in the U.S. State
Department from 1984 to 1988. He lives in Brussels with
his wife and two children.

A NOTE ON THE TYPE

This book was set in Minion, a typeface produced by the Adobe Corporation specifically for the Macintosh personal computer and released in 1990. Designed by Robert Slimbach, Minion combines the classic characteristics of old-style faces with the full complement of weights required for modern typesetting.

Composed by Creative Graphics,
Allentown, Pennsylvania
Printed and bound by R. R. Donnelley,
Crawfordsville, Indiana
Designed by Virginia Tan